TWENTIETH CENTURY INTERPRETATIONS

The aim of this series is to present the best in contemporary critical opinion on major authors, providing a twentieth century perspective on their
changing status in an era of profound revaluation.

Maynard Mack, *Series Editor*
Yale University

THE GLASS MENAGERIE

A COLLECTION OF CRITICAL ESSAYS

Edited by
R. B. Parker

Prentice-Hall, Inc.

A SPECTRUM BOOK

Englewood Cliffs, N.J.

Library of Congress Cataloging in Publication Data
Main entry under title:

Twentieth century interpretations of The glass menagerie.

(Twentieth century interpretations)
"A Spectrum Book."
Bibliography: p.
1. Williams, Tennessee, 1911–1983.   The glass
menagerie—Addresses, essays, lectures.   I. Parker, R. B.
II. Williams, Tennessee, 1911–1983.   The glass
menagerie.   III. Series.
PS3545.I53.5G538 1983   812'.54   83–3380
ISBN 0-13-934836-0
ISBN 0-13-934828-X (pbk.)

ISBN 0-13-934836-0

ISBN 0-13-934828-X {PBK.}

Editorial production supervision by Maxine Bartow and Marlys Lehmann
Cover woodengraving by Vivian Berger © 1983
Manufacturing buyer: Cathie Lenard

Prentice-Hall International, Inc., *London*
Prentice-Hall of Australia Pty. Limited, *Sydney*
Prentice-Hall Canada Inc., *Toronto*
Prentice-Hall of India Private Limited, *New Delhi*
Prentice-Hall of Japan, Inc., *Tokyo*
Prentice-Hall of Southeast Asia Pte. Ltd., *Singapore*
Whitehall Books Limited, *Wellington, New Zealand*
Editora Prentice-Hall do Brasil Ltda., *Rio de Janeiro*

For Lorraine d'Agincourt and Peter Canning

Contents

III. Characters and Themes

IV. Dramaturgy

Acknowledgments

Acknowledgment is gratefully made to Random House, Inc., for permission to reprint excerpts from the "Reading Edition" of *The Glass Menagerie* by Tennessee Williams (© 1945 by Random House Ltd.); to International Creative Management (for the author) for permission to reprint excerpts from the "Acting Edition" of *The Glass Menagerie* (©1948 by Tennessee Williams and Edwina D. Williams); to Doubleday and Co., Inc., for permission to reprint excerpts from *Memoirs* by Tennessee Williams (© 1972, 1975 by Tennessee Williams); and to New Directions Publishing Corporation (for the authors) for permission to reprint from the following:

One Arm and Other Stories, Copyright © 1948 by Tennessee Williams.

Hard Candy, Copyright © 1954 by Tennessee Williams.

In the Winter of Cities, Copyright © 1956 by Tennessee Williams.

You Touched Me, Copyright © 1939 by Story Magazine, Inc., Copyright © 1966 by Tennessee Williams.

Where I Live, Copyright © 1978 by Tennessee Williams.

Introduction

R. B. Parker

Stage History

Tennessee Williams was already thirty-four when *The Glass Menagerie* had its brilliant Broadway opening at the Playhouse Theatre on March 31, 1945. *Menagerie* was his sixth or seventh full-length play, not counting numerous one-acters, poems, and short stories. He had won a Group Theatre award in 1939 for *American Blues,* a collection of three short, social-protest plays; and this had led to a Rockefeller grant, followed, in turn, by a Theatre Guild production of his *Battle of Angels,* which closed quickly in Boston during its pre-Broadway tryout. In 1940 American sensibilities were clearly not ready for the sex and violence of what was to become known as Williams' "southern gothic," and this early failure undoubtedly had an influence on the much more muted tone of *The Glass Menagerie* to follow.

After *Battle of Angels* Williams returned to the wandering, bohemian life he had been leading since leaving his home in St. Louis in 1938, working at a series of low-paying jobs across the country while he stubbornly, sometimes desperately continued to write. He was earning only fifteen dollars a week as a cinema usher in New York when in May 1943 his agent, Audrey Wood, secured him a six-month contract as a writer with Metro-Goldwyn-Mayer. Predictably, Williams soon ran foul of Hollywood taste and was suspended by the studio for refusing to write for a child star, but the apparent disaster turned to his advantage because it left him free to work at what he pleased for the duration of his contract.

For some time he had been struggling to absorb painful family experience into various literary forms—short stories, one-acters, and two full-length plays of different scope, both called *The Gentleman Caller*—and out of this larger work in progress he now redrafted a short story, "Portrait of a Girl in Glass" (printed in *One Arm and Other Stories* (1948), 95–112) and a screenplay also called *The*

Gentleman Caller. MGM turned the screenplay down, so Williams reworked the material yet again, turning it back into a stage play, and sent it off, a little deprecatingly, to his agent in New York. This was *The Glass Menagerie,* though probably it acquired that title only at a later stage, during the Chicago tryout.[1]

Audrey Wood took Williams' script to Eddie Dowling, an independent actor-director-producer who had recently been successful with William Saroyan's *The Time of Your Life.* Although at fifty-three Dowling was really too old for the role, he decided to act the part of Tom himself; he cast Julie Haydon, his lead in the Saroyan, as Laura, and Anthony Ross as Jim; and for the crucial role of the mother, Amanda, he gambled on Laurette Taylor, a forgotten star who was trying to make a comeback after alcoholism. Margo Jones agreed to co-direct; Jo Mielziner was signed up as designer; Paul Bowles wrote special music; a businessman called Louis J. Singer, who ran a chain of second-string hotels and had never invested in theatre before (and was never to do so again), was persuaded to be co-producer; and Dowling decided to open at Chicago's Civic Theatre.

At first, Williams seemed bound for another disaster. Under the influence of the New York critic George Jean Nathan, Dowling and Singer pressed for substantial alterations in the script, which Williams, with the debacle of *Battle of Angels* in mind, found increasingly difficult to resist. Laurette Taylor feuded with Dowling and seemed unable to memorize her lines or catch the proper southern accent. The set took twenty-four hours to erect because the supervisor got drunk and disappeared. Julie Haydon's dress turned out to be the wrong color for the lighting; and just before the curtain rose for the first performance on December 26, 1944, Laurette Taylor was found redyeing the old bathrobe she had to wear in the second act.

Nevertheless, the opening was a triumph, with Miss Taylor suddenly revealing an extraordinarily touching brilliance. Reviews were enthusiastic, but the box office continued to be sluggish, and Singer became convinced they had a flop on their hands. By the end of the first week the producers would have closed the play[2] except for a campaign on its behalf by the Chicago critics led by Claudia Cassidy of the *Tribune,* and in another week the theater had begun to sell out. By the time it reached New York, *The Glass Menagerie's* reputation had preceded it, and its triumphal opening on Broadway was assured. It continued at the Playhouse for 563 performances, won the *Billboard*-sponsored Donaldson Award, the Sidney Howard Memorial Award, and the fourth annual award of the Catholic monthly, *The Sign,* and was selected by the New York Drama Critics as the best American play of the 1944–45 season.

Laurette Taylor herself won the Antoinette Perry award as the season's best actress, and several reviewers were inclined to attribute the play's success mainly to her performance until other productions confirmed the brilliance of the script itself. It was quickly successful in Basel, Rome, Paris, Stockholm, and London (where Helen Hayes played Amanda), and Warner Brothers outbid Williams' old employer MGM and in 1950 released a rather botched film version with a star-studded but inappropriate cast. A revival at the New York City Center in 1956, with Helen Hayes repeating Amanda, enjoyed the longest Broadway run of any American play revival during the preceding twenty-five years; the Theatre Guild's American Repertory Company took it on a European and South American tour in 1961; another Broadway revival with Maureen Stapleton as Amanda ran for 175 performances in 1965; and it was revived successfully again at the Circle-in-the-Square Theatre in 1975–76, with Maureen Stapleton once more playing Amanda. There have been two television versions, one by CBS-TV in 1966 with Shirley Booth as Amanda, the other by ABC-TV in 1973 with Katharine Hepburn; and in November 1980 Julie Haydon, the original Laura, returned as Amanda in a production at the Lion Theatre on West 42nd Street. The play is also constantly performed by amateur and academic groups and has become a standard teaching text. Its success has ensured that the half-share in royalties that Williams immediately signed over to his mother kept her in comfortable independence for the rest of her life.

Autobiographical Elements

Although Mrs. Edwina Williams has pointed out the many differences between the Williams family and the Wingfields,[3] and Gilbert Debusscher has shown the play's indebtedness to Hart Crane (pp. 31–43), *The Glass Menagerie* is nonetheless Tennessee Williams' most autobiographical play, accurate to the imaginative reality of his experience even when it departs from fact in detail. An understanding of this background can therefore be helpful in appreciating its achievement.

Williams' parents were badly mismatched. Cornelius Coffin Williams was a traveling salesman, aggressively and self-consciously masculine, accustomed to the hard drinking, profane camaraderie of the road; Edwina Dakin was the high-strung, prudish daughter of an Episcopalian rector, used to social deference and a life of conscious refinement. They clashed early in their marriage; and as "C. C." was usually traveling, Mrs. Williams raised her first two children, Thomas Lanier, born in 1911, and Rose, two years his elder, at her father's various Mississippi rectories. Williams remembers these first eight years as a sort of paradise lost. His grandfather was a serene, gentle man (sketched later as Nonno in *Night of the Iguana*), and young Tom's life revolved around Mrs. Dakin, whom he called "Grand," his mother, and particularly Rose, a pretty, imaginative child who was his constant companion: "We were exclusive, so close to each other we had no need of others".[4] An attack of diptheria that kept him out of school for a year and briefly paralyzed his legs (a disability he transfers to Laura in the play) increased this sense of sheltered apartness.

In 1918, however, C. C. was promoted to a managerial position by his firm, the International Shoe Company, and moved the family to an apartment in St. Louis. "It was a tragic move," Williams records. "Neither my sister nor I could adjust ourselves to life in a Midwestern city".[5] They were depressed by their "perpetually dim little apartment in a wilderness of identical brick and concrete structures with no grass and no trees nearer than the park," humiliated by feeling poor and no longer receiving the deference accorded to rectory children, and appalled by the aggressiveness of city life. C. C.'s continual presence was an added source of tension, particularly for Tom because his father considered him effeminate; and a long visit that he made to his grandparents in 1919, after the birth of his brother Dakin, only made the contrast with his own home seem more bitter.

At first these circumstances threw Tom and his sister even closer together and her bedroom became their special haven. The savagery of the city was epitomized for them by a neighboring alley in which dogs would corner and kill cats—a detail included in "Portrait of a Girl in Glass" but omitted from *Menagerie*—so that Rose kept the shade drawn over her window. To relieve the half-light the children painted her furniture white, put up white curtains, and on shelves around the room Rose placed her collection of glass ornaments, mostly little animals, which came to represent "all the small and tender things that relieve the austere pattern of life and make it endurable to the sensitive."[6] These figurines were also associated by Williams with parish visits he had made with his grandfather to a lady named Laura Young:

> . . . she was something green and cool in a sulphurous landscape. But there was a shadow upon her. For that reason we called upon her more frequently than anyone else. She loved me. I adored her. She lived in a white house near an orchard and in an arch between two rooms were hung some pendants of glass that were a thousand colors. That is a prism, she said. She lifted me and told me to shake them. When I did, they made a delicate music.[7]

With puberty, however, the closeness of Williams' relation to Rose changed. In one of his short stories, "The Resemblance Between a Violin Case and a Coffin" (*Hard Candy*, 1954), he conveys his bewildered irritation at Rose's sudden remoteness, poignantly understood in retrospect in part 3 of his poem "Recuerdo" (*In the Winter of Cities*, 1956, p. 80):

> At fifteen my sister
> no longer waited for me,
> impatiently at the White Star Pharmacy corner
> but plunged headlong
> into the discovery, Love!
> Then vanished completely—
> for love's explosion, defined as early madness
> consumingly shone in her transparent heart for a season
> and burned it out, a tissue-paper lantern!
>
> My sister was quicker at everything than I.

Rose gradually retreated into a private mental world that was to end in schizophrenia. In his *Memoirs* (1975) Williams claims that she was a normal but highly sexed girl destroyed by the opposing pressures of her mother's puritanism (p. 119) and C. C.'s improprieties (pp. 124–25); but he also blames himself because he paid less and less attention to his sister as his own sexual awakening began, especially after he became aware in college of his inclinations toward homosexuality.

The situation worsened when poor grades provoked C. C. to withdraw his son from the University of Missouri in his junior year and to find him a dead-end job like Tom Wingfield's with the International Shoe Company. Williams used to escape to the factory roof to smoke and gaze across the Mississippi, like the hero of another of his plays about this time, *Stairs to the Roof;* and night after night he chain-smoked and drank black coffee in his bedroom, trying to write. After two years his health collapsed; his leg paralysis returned, and the family doctor insisted that he leave the shoe factory. This breakdown coincided, Williams claims, with Rose's first overt aberration: "I remember her wandering into my small room and saying 'Let's die together'." (*Memoirs,* p. 39)

After recuperation, Williams enrolled at George Washington University in St. Louis. There he read intensively—especially Chekhov, Hart Crane, and (like Tom Wingfield) D. H. Lawrence—and, under the stimulus of a group called the Mummers Theatre, he began to concentrate on writing plays. He again flunked his course work, however, and in 1937 had to transfer to a playwriting course at the University of Iowa in order to finish his B.A. It was during this rackety college period that his sister's mental crisis occurred. As in the play, Mrs. Williams tried vainly to combat Rose's withdrawal by a disastrous secretarial course and by persuading Tom to invite his friends to the house for company[8]; and in *Memoirs* Williams says he feels guilty about his lack of concern for Rose at the time: "It's not pleasant to look back on that year [1937] and to know that Rose knew she was going mad and to know, also, that I wasn't too kind to my sister" (p. 121). He tells of her tattling on a wild party he gave at the house during their parents' absence, in revenge for which he hissed at her on the stairs, "I hate the sight of your ugly old face," leaving her stricken and wordless, crouched against the wall. "This is the cruelest thing I have done in my life, I suspect," he comments, "for which I can never properly atone." (p. 122) Later that year Rose was put in an institution; and in the summer, while Williams was away with some of his new friends, his parents gave their permission for the frontal lobotomy that rendered Rose harmless but childish for the rest of her life.

Rose's tragedy was a traumatic experience for Williams from which he never freed himself. It seems closely related to his feeling that love leads inevitably to loss and betrayal, as reflected in such poems as "Cortege" and "The Comforter and Betrayer" (*In the Winter of Cities,* 53, 44). The pattern is extraordinarily clear in *Suddenly Last Summer,* written in the late 1950s after psychoanalysis, in which the heroine is threatened with lobotomy for discovering the homosexuality of her cousin; but as Clayton's essay demonstrates (pp. 109–19), an ambiguous brother–sister relationship recurs throughout Williams' work. His most important recent play, known variously as *Out Cry* or *The Two Character Play,* deals with the same subject, and has been described as "in some ways like a sequel to *The Glass Menagerie*";[9] and, fittingly, the last pages of *Memoirs* express his concern with releasing his sister from her institution to end her days in a house he has bought for her near his own at Key West.

It is worth noting, moreover, that Williams blames his mother and himself for Rose's disaster more than his father. Despite the harsh treatment he received from C. C., he shows a surprising sympathy for his father, and in a biography-in-progress his brother Dakin reports him as blaming their mother's prudery for driving C. C. from home, and comments that "According to Tom, Dad would have been completely justified in doing to Edwina exactly what the father has done to the mother in *Glass Menagerie.*"[10] When Williams graduated from Iowa in 1938 and struck out on his own, he substituted "Tennessee" for "Thomas Lanier" because he saw himself adventuring like his father's family who had helped to pioneer Tennessee; and as Tom Wingfield's flight in *Glass Menagerie* repeats that of the father "who fell in love with long distance," so Williams credits C. C. for his own creative restlessness and energy.

Critical Approaches

Besides exploring this autobiographical dimension, early criticism of *The Glass Menagerie* tends to concentrate with varying degrees of success on psychological and moral evaluation of the characters. One of the best examples of the approach is Benjamin Nelson's chapter on the play from his *Tennessee Williams, The Man and His Work* (1961: see pp. 87–95), which concentrates on the ambiguities of Jim O'Connor, Tom, and especially Amanda. Nelson is working from the "reading text" of the play, and it is interesting to put his analysis of Amanda against James L. Rowland's article, "Tennessee's Two Amandas" (see pp. 62–74), which shows how most of these ambiguities have been pruned from the "acting text," so that Amanda emerges as a much more sympathetic character. Nelson's study reveals a very important aspect of Williams' work, however: his belief in the essential ambivalence of human behaviour:

> . . . the thing that I've always pushed in my writing—that I've always felt needed to be said over and over—[is] that human relations are terrifyingly ambiguous. If you write a character that isn't ambiguous you are writing a false character, not a true one.[11]

In *Menagerie* this ambivalence is focused in the way that all the characters try to avoid confronting unpleasant truths. Such escapism is seen as a weakness, and in the case of Jim and Amanda is rendered comically, but we are also clearly meant to sympathize with it; and it is important to recognize that it encompasses not only the young Tom, escaping into daydreams and the movies, but also the Tom who is remembering, the wanderer forever trying to evade his past. Without such a balance, the play can easily degenerate into sentimentality.

Once the pattern had been clarified two years later by Alma in *Summer and Smoke* and Blanche in *A Streetcar Named Desire,* it became common to interpret Amanda in relation to the myth of the American South before the Civil War, that tradition of a lost world of aristocratic elegance and honor. Signi Falk adopts this approach in her chapter "The Southern Gentlewoman" (*Tennessee Williams.* New York: Twayne, 1961), and, though there is no study as complex as Thomas E. Porter's chapter on *Streetcar* in *Myth and Modern American Drama* (1969), there are interesting essays by Peggy Prenshawe, Jacob H. Adler, and Joseph K. Davis that touch on *Menagerie* from this point of view in Jac Tharpe's anthology, *Tennessee Williams: A Tribute* (1977).

Besides the myth of the South, *The Glass Menagerie* has also been approached thematically from political, psychological, and religious angles. Williams is not really a political writer, of course: He has said, "I don't deal with social problems, because those are not the problems that move me. . . . My politics is that of the heart. I am only interested in human nature." Nonetheless, it is worth remembering that in his early years he tried several times to get into the W.P.A. writers project, and the crucial recognition of his work, the prize that set his career going, was a Group Theatre award for his trilogy of social protest plays, *American Blues.* Certainly, as Grigor Pavlov's "A Comparative Study of Tennessee Williams' *The Glass Menagerie* and *Portrait of a Girl in Glass*" demonstrates (*Annuaire de l'Université de Sofia, Faculté des Lettres,* Vol. LXII. 1 (1968), 113–131), a comparison of "Portrait" and *Menagerie* reveals that the latter has a dimension of social comment quite lacking in the short story, and this comment is one that is critical of conditions that led to the Depression, the Spanish Civil War, and World War II. Gilbert Debusscher's response to Pavlov in "Tennessee Williams' Unicorn" (*Revue belge de Philologie et d'Histoire,* 49, 1971, 875–85) quite justly protests against his overemphasis on this one aspect of the play to the exclusion of more important dimensions, such as the religious symbolism analysed by Roger Stein (see pp. 134–42); but, as Stein himself points out in an afterword to his article, the social element Pavlov is concerned with is demonstrably *in* the play and is not to be ignored.

Of the psychological approaches to *Menagerie,* the earliest were discussions of Williams' use of neurotic heroines (eg., Constantin N. Stavrou, "The Neurotic Heroine in Tennessee Williams," *Literature and Psychology,* 5, 1955, 26–34), but much more basic is Tom Scanlan's analysis of the play in terms of traditional American attitudes to the family (see pp. 96–108)—the simultaneous reliance on the family unit for meaning and values yet the contradictory need to repudiate and escape it: an approach that catches the ambivalence of Tom Wingfield's nostalgia very accurately. More narrowly focused, but fascinating for its relation to Williams' work as a whole, is John Strother Clayton's exploration of the special importance of the brother–sister symbiosis in the play (pp. 109–19). Though there is no need to push this to the point of clinical incest, as in Daniel Dervin's "The Spook in the Rainforest: the incestuous structure of Tennessee Williams' plays" (*Psychocultural Review,* 3, 1979, 153–183)—in fact, Williams specifically says, "My sister and I had a close relationship, quite unsullied by carnal knowledge. . . . And yet our love was, and is, the deepest of our lives and was, perhaps, very pertinent to our withdrawal from extra-familial attachments. . . ." (*Memoirs,* p. 119)—his continued concern with this relationship is confirmed by the variously entitled *Out Cry* (1973) or *The Two Character Play* (1967, 1975), which Williams describes as "the big one. . . . close to the marrow of my bones" (*Memoirs,* pp. 129, 228); and this suggests that the interdependence of Tom and Laura warrants more critical consideration than has been given it in the past, particularly in relation to the ambiguities of tone at the conclusion.

Roger Stein's demonstration of the metaphysical (or, more precisely, existentialist) dimension to *Menagerie* implicit in its use of religious symbolism—further details of which are added by De-busscher, "Williams' Unicorn", and Judith Thompson, "Symbol-ism, Myth, and Ritual in *The Glass Menagerie, The Rose Tattoo,* and *Orpheus Descending*" (Tharpe, 685–693)—combines thematic inter-pretation with an analysis of techniques that move the play beyond the mainly realistic psychological–sociological approaches of the earlier Williams critics. In this technical analysis, verbal and theatrical devices are usually considered together—as in Esther Jackson's important pioneering study, *The Broken World of Tennessee Williams* (1965), which is still the most sustained argument for a nonrealist approach to Williams' art—and there has been com-paratively little work done specifically on the verbal texture of the play. Ruby Cohn touches on the implications of a desperate overfacility with words in a chapter entitled "Tennessee Williams' Garrulous Grotesques" in her book *Dialogue in American Drama* (1971); and drawing on his experience acting the role, Thomas King illuminates important ironic elements and shifts of tone in Tom's soliloquies that complicate their emotional effect (see pp. 75–86); while Frank Durham has a short but interesting comment on the use of stichomythia and other speech patternings in the play (see pp. 120–33). Durham sets this patterning in relation to other, non-verbal aspects of the dramaturgy, however, and like most technical analyses of *Menagerie,* spends more time on its manipulation of theatrical effects than on its language proper.

It is perhaps inevitable that this should be so because Williams' "Production Notes" to *Menagerie* emphasize the importance of what he calls "plastic theatre"—that is, metaphoric or symbolic use of such nonverbal elements of production as stage setting, props, lighting, and sound. These techniques have been traced variously to expressionism (eg., Mary Ann Corrigan, "Beyond Verisimilitude: Echoes of Expressionism in Williams' Plays", in Tharpe, pp. 375–412) and symbolism (eg., June Bennett Larsen, "Tennessee Williams: Optimistic Symbolist," Tharpe, 413–28), but most interesting, considering Williams' work for MGM at the time he wrote the play and the importance of movies as Tom's avenue of escape within *Menagerie* itself (which Williams has said reflects his own behavior as a young man), is the identification of "plastic" technique with cinematic effects. One of the pioneers of this approach was George Brandt ("Cinematic structure in the work of Tennessee Williams," in *American Theatre,* ed. J. R. Brown and B. Harris, 1967, pp. 163–187), whose work is incorporated and extended by Frank Durham (pp. 120–33); and a more recent discussion can be found in Gene Phillips, *The Films of Tennessee Williams* (1980), where an analysis of cinematic technique in the play itself is combined with discussion of its movie and television adaptations—in which, ironically, as Maurice Yacowar shows about the movie version, most of the subtleties of Williams' technique are sacrificed to more stock and sentimental effects (see pp. 26–30). The importance of these nonrealist techniques, of course, as Paul Nolan's article emphasizes (see pp. 143–52), is that they establish *The Glass Menagerie* not as a slice of life that the audience can watch objectively but as a static "memory play," seen only through the temperament of Tom, who looks back with an ambivalent mixture of nostalgia, regret, guilt, and self-justification. Thus, Nolan very interestingly suggests, the relation set up with the audience in a "memory play" is distinct from either the "objectivity" associated with realism or the "identi-fication" demanded by full expressionism.

The importance of this perspective can perhaps be most illumi-natingly demonstrated by what has become the central critical controversy about *Menagerie:* whether or not the slide projections should be used. These were cut out of the original production (and from the Dramatists Playservice "acting edition" based on it, which has become the text for most subsequent productions), but were restored by Williams himself in the so-called "reading edition" published by Random House and New Directions. Early com-mentators uniformly agreed with Eddie Dowling that the pro-jections were best omitted, and this is still the opinion of some more recent critics (e.g., Lester Beaurline, "The Director, the Script, and Author's Revisions: A Critical Problem," in *Papers in Dramatic Theory and Criticism,* ed. David M. Knauf, 1969, p. 89; S. Alan Chessler, "Tennessee Williams: Reassessment and Assessment," in Tharpe, p. 853; Mary Ann Corrigan, "Beyond Verisimilitude," in Tharpe, p. 392). Nor is it hard to understand this position. In the early 1940s American audiences were familiar with realism and theatricality separately but not with the tension between them on which *Menagerie* depends; the first production was so successful that it is hardly surprising that critics should assume that the projections must have been redundant; and Williams' justification in his "Production Notes," which argues that the projections clarify dramatic structure, is unpersuasive. Williams also suggests another function, however, that is crucial but was largely ignored, perhaps because of the vagueness of its phrasing: "I think the screen will have a definite emotional appeal, less definable but just as important."

The theatricalism seems to have three main functions, in fact: It serves to maintain an ironic distance between the early Tom-within-the-play and the later Tom-remembering; its element of jaunty black humor can also be seen as a way that Tom tries to protect himself from the pain and guilt of his nostalgia; and, most subtly of all, it creates a slightly abrasive distance between Tom and the audience—particularly in the way that several of the projections seem to parody reactions by Laura (e.g., "Not Jim," "Terror," "Gentleman caller waving goodbye—gaily"), a character who is otherwise presented as wholly sympathetic. The emotional perception of such discordances determines whether one sees the action of the play (with Scanlan) as essentially a reenactment in which, like the characters of Sartre's *Huis Clos* (which Williams greatly admires: cf. *Memoirs,* p. 149), Tom remains emotionally trapped within a painfully ambiguous situation, or, alternatively, as an exorcism by which he comes to terms with his past and manages to win free from it—a position argued most forthrightly by Thomas E. Scheye in *"The Glass Menagerie:* 'It's no tragedy, Freckles' " (Tharpe, pp. 207–13). If the play is seen as reenactment, then Tom is once more guilty of abandoning his sister (as his command to her "Blow out your candles" repeats, within the play, his earlier plunging of the stage into darkness by selfishly misappropriating the family's electricity payment); and it can be argued that the uneasy jocularity of some of the projections and the element of overpoeticism in Tom's final soliloquies (which Williams himself remarks on in *Memoirs,* p. 84) reflect not only regret and remorse but also a self-lacerating awareness that by abandoning Laura he is repudiating an essential part of himself—just as the brother and sister in *The Two Character Play* end in a pact of mutual destruction that Williams calls a "liebestod," and that he represents by the same symbolic device as in *Menagerie* of blacking out the stage. It seems pertinent, therefore, that in early letters to his friend Donald Windham, Williams explains that *The Gentleman Caller* "lacks the violence that excites me, so I piddle around with it," and vows "It is the *last* play I will write for the *now* existing theatre".[12] The missing sex and violence that seem to set *The Glass Menagerie* apart from the rest of Williams' canon are, in fact, adumbrated in the complex tone produced by the original theatricalism and the element of exaggeration—of deliberate forcing—in the style of Tom's addresses to the audience.

This argument for the superiority of the "reading version" of the play to the "acting text" can also, to some extent, be supported by a final critical approach—the study of *Menagerie*'s development by comparison to other Williams' versions of the story. At first such comparisons were limited to other versions in print—Pavlov's comparison of *Menagerie* to the short story "Portrait of a Girl in Glass," for instance, or comparisons of the published acting version and the reading version of the play by James Rowland, showing the more sympathetic picture of Amanda in the former, and by Thomas King, showing the more ironic nature of Tom's soliloquies in the latter;[13] but of recent years it has also become possible to examine Williams' working drafts of the play. Lester Beaurline's lucid appraisal of the Williams manuscripts in the Barrett library of the University of Virginia (see pp. 44–52) pioneered this approach by distinguishing at least four stages in the development of the text; but since his essay appeared, a great deal of extra material has been deposited at the Humanities Centre of the University of Texas that suggests that the genesis of the play was even more complex than Beaurline supposed, and that the reading version is a far more accurate reflection of Williams' full intention than the acting script, though the latter may very well continue to be the better version to stage (see Parker, pp. 53–61).

This problem cannot begin to be resolved, however, until the Texas archive is more thoroughly sorted and has been collated with the draft material in Virginia; and, even then, interpretation will probably rely as much upon a critic's personal reaction to the ambivalence of the play as on objective textual evidence. Like a more detailed investigation of *The Glass Menagerie*'s language, or a fuller consideration of the audience dynamic established by its peculiar "memory play" form, the genesis of the text remains a promising area for further research and criticism. Despite the good work already done, scholarship on Tennessee Williams is still only just beginning.

Notes

[1]See Debusscher, "Menagerie, Glass and Wine: Tennessee Williams and Hart Crane", pp. 31–43.

[2]William Inge describes the producers' hostility and Williams' depression at this time: See Mike Steen, *A Look at Tennessee Williams* (New York: Hawthorn, 1969), 93–123.

[3]Edwina Williams and Lucy Freeman, *Remember Me to Tom* (New York: G.P. Putnam's Sons, 1963), pp. 149, 174–5.

[4]Williams, quoted in "The Life and Ideas of Tennessee Williams", *New York PM Magazine* (May 6, 1945), p. 6; cf. *Memoirs,* pp. 11–12.

[5]"Facts About Me," in *Where I Live,* ed. Christine R. Day and Bob Woods (New York: New Directions, 1978), p. 59.

[6]Williams, quoted in Lincoln Barnett,"Tennessee Williams", *Life* 24 (Feb. 16, 1948), 118.

[7]Quoted in Paul Moor, "A Mississippian Named Tennessee," *Harper's Magazine* 197 (July 1948), 164.

[8]The poet Clark Mills Burney recalls such a visit in Gene Phillips, *The Films of Tennessee Williams* (East Brunswick, N.J.: Associated University Presses, 1980), p. 47.

[9]Peggy Prenshawe, "The Paradoxical Southern World of Tennessee Williams," in *Tennessee Williams: A Tribute,* ed. Jac Tharpe (Jackson: University Press of Mississippi, 1977), p. 55.

[10]Quoted in Phillips, p. 40.

[11]Williams, in Lewis Funke and John E. Booth, "Williams on Williams," *Theatre Arts,* 46 (January 1962), p. 18.

[12]Donald Windham, ed., *Tennessee Williams' Letters to Donald Windham, 1940–1965* (1977), pp. 94, 148. Cf. Williams' comment in an early interview with *Time:* "In *The Glass Menagerie* I said all the nice things I have to say about people. The future things will be harsher". *Time* (April 23, 1945), p. 88.

[13]Cf. also: Charles S. Watson, "The Revision of *The Glass Menagerie:* The Passing of Good Manners," *Southern Literary Journal* 8 (Spring 1978), 74–8; and the brief but illuminating comparison to an earlier one-acter, *The Last Goodbye,* in George Niesen, "The Artist against Reality in the Plays of Tennessee Williams," in Tharpe, pp. 466–68.

The First Production
of *The Glass Menagerie*

Stark Young

Of all our actors, certainly of all those who have become known, Miss Laurette Taylor could not be called the most cultured, the most versatile in diverse styles, the most gracious-minded, but few would deny that she is the most talented. She is the real and first talent of them all. She has been largely absent from the stage during so many years that her return is an event and everybody knows it. It turns out, in *The Glass Menagerie,* to be a triumph as well. So is the rôle she plays.

Miss Taylor's rôle in Mr. Williams' play is that of a frowsy, aging woman who lives with her son and daughter, in a flat off a St. Louis alley. It is a far cry from the Deep South, where her girlhood was spent and her memories dwell, and where she has refused the rich planters' sons because she lost her heart to a man who worked for the telephone company and whose smile misled everybody. The daughter is a cripple, too shy and hurt and vague ever to have got through school. She spends her time playing old phonograph records that her father had left behind when he abandoned her mother and went away for good, and collecting glass animals— hence the title of the play. The son is a failure, discontented with his job in the warehouse, vaguely itching to write poetry, and longing to roam the world. The mother worships, nags, scolds and tries to do her best by her children. Finally, when she thinks it is time her daughter got married, she plagues the son into bringing a man home with him; he brings a friend from the warehouse. The visitor, impressed though he is with the daughter, turns out to be already in love and engaged.

In the end the son follows his father's example and goes off to

"The First Production of *The Glass Menagerie*" (editor's title) by Stark Young. From *The New Republic,* 112 (April 16, 1945), 505. Copyright © 1945 Stark Young. Reprinted by permission of the Stark Young estate.

make his way wandering the world. The scheme of *The Glass Menagerie* includes a Narrator, who opens the play and appears between the scenes from time to time (to follow "the part of the sun"). If properly followed, which it is not in the production, this is a very imaginative motif on the dramatist's part, this subtle identification of the father with the son, the son with the father.

This rôle is played by the actor who takes the part of the son. The story, as we see it on the stage, all happens in the son's mind long afterward, and in the last narration, a kind of epilogue, we are told that in the midst of the years and in far, strange places, wherever he goes, he can never lose the image of his sister there at home; all things bring her back to him.

What Miss Laurette Taylor does with these matters can be at least partially imagined if you know the quality of her special gift. This, even after just seeing the play, is almost impossible to convey with anything like the full, wonderful truth. Hers is naturalistic acting of the most profound, spontaneous, unbroken continuity and moving life. There is an inexplicable rightness, moment by moment, phrase by phrase, endlessly varied in the transitions. Technique, which is always composed of skill and instinct working together, is in this case so overlaid with warmth, tenderness and wit that any analysis is completely baffled. Only a trained theatre eye and ear can tell what is happening, and then only at times. Miss Laurette Taylor is capable of a performance so right and perfect that you do not even think of it as a great performance. I do not mean to go into a kind of Seidletz hysterics to make my point about what she does with this rôle in *The Glass Menagerie,* I merely say that it has a characteristic of seeming beyond any contrivance and of a sort of changing rhythm of translucence rarely to be seen in the theatre. The one short-coming about this portrayal of the mother is that Miss Taylor does not achieve the quality of the aristocrat, however broken down and wasted and lost, that Mr. Williams intended. She is astonishingly Southern, partly due to the writing and partly to her ready intuition of feeling, tone and climax; but in an elusive sense that would be impossible to convey, and that any Southerner of Mr. Williams' class would understand almost automatically, she is not what is implied in the play. No use in wasting time on that point; if she had been so, had been the broken-down aristocrat that Mr. Williams wrote, the effect would have been largely lost on most audiences, and as things went the play got on very well without it.

But true as all this may be of Miss Taylor, we must not let that blind us to the case of the play itself and of the whole occasion. The play gives every one of the four characters that it presents a glowing, rich opportunity, genuine emotional motivations, a rhythm of situations that are alive, and speech that is fresh, living, abundant and free of stale theatre diction. The author is not awed by the usual sterilities of our play-writing patterns. On the other hand he is too imaginative, genuine, or has too much good taste, to be coy about the free devices on which his play is built, a true, rich talent, unpredictable like all true talents, an astute stage sense, an intense, quivering clarity, all light and feeling once the intelligence of it is well anchored—a talent, too, I should say, that New York will buy tickets for in later plays, especially if enough of the sexy is added to things, but will never quite understand.

The Glass Menagerie appears to drag, or go slow, at times, though I am not sure about this and certainly found it less so than a number of people I have heard speak of it. These slow places occur in the Narrator portions and sometimes in the scenes between mother and son. In my opinion this may be almost entirely due to the fact that Mr. Eddie Dowling does not let himself go enough to make you believe that he is the son of such a mother or such a father. We have no ready, or vivid, sense that he longs to wander, to write poetry—I even forgot to remember what he was working at when he sat before the papers on the table, supposed, however, to be bent on a poem. Mr. Dowling speaks his Narrator scenes plainly and serviceably, with the result that they are made to seem to be a mistake on the playwright's part, a mistake to include them at all; for they seem extraneous and tiresome in the midst of the play's emotional current. And many critics will speak of them as such. This is not the case at all. It is curious that an actor of Mr. Dowling's experience and showmanship should pass up thus a rôle where the dramatist's invention is really so striking and, for that matter, so useful to the player. If these speeches were spoken with variety, impulse and intensity, as if the son himself were speaking—which is what happens really, since the play is a dream within his memory—if they were spoken as if they were from a born wanderer and adventurer, a chip off the old block, wild-headed like his father—and like his mother for that matter, for she too had wandered far from home indeed—the whole of the Narrator would be another matter entirely, it would be truly a part of the story. Thus Mr.

Dowling does much harm to the play. The fact remains, nevertheless, that he is sure to be praised for his playing of the role, on the
basis that it is poised and not exaggerated—such is the irony of the
acting art and its observers.

To say, as Mr. Nichols does in his review in the *New York Times* that
there are such unconnected things with the story as "snatches of talk
about the war, bits of psychology, occasional moments of rather
florid writing" is mistaken indeed. The part Miss Taylor plays is,
quite aside from her rendering of it, the best written rôle that I have
seen in a play for years. All the language and all the motifs are free
and true; I recognized them inch by inch, and I should know, for I
came from the same part of the country, the same locality and life,
in fact, that Mr. Williams does. Such a response and attitude as that
Mr. Nichols expresses is the kind of thing that helps to tie our
theatre down. It is the application of Times Square practical
knowledge, the kind of thing that makes, to take one instance, the
writing, the talk, in *The Late George Apley* so sterile and so little like the
Boston it assumes to be. One of the things most needed in the
theatre is a sense of language, a sense of texture in speech, vibration
and impulse in speech. Behind the Southern speech in the mother's
part is the echo of great literature, or at least a respect for it. There is
the sense in it of her having been born out of a tradition, not out of a
box. It has echo and the music of it. The mother's characterization
is both appalling and human, both cold and loving. No role could
be more realistically written than this, but it has the variety,
suddenness, passion and freedom, almost unconscious freedom
perhaps, of true realism.

Miss Julie Haydon gave one of her translucent performances of a
dreaming, wounded, half-out-of-this-world young girl. Mr. Anthony Ross, as the visitor, for whom the author has written a long
and excellent scene, original and tender, with the girl, played
admirably.

Mr. Jo Mielziner did the complicated setting for *The Glass
Menagerie,* streets at the side, a front room, a back room, a wall
shutting them off when needed. The scene is effectively ingenious.
But even though the story happens in a dream and vagueness may
be called for, I see no reason why the color should be quite so dull.
For example, it was only by a most creditable leap of the
imagination that one could make out that the enlarged photograph
of the vanished father on the wall was really that of Mr. Dowling, the

son. The result was that a notable motivation on the part of the dramatist, which is that the son, the Narrator, and the father are all one and the same, was all but lost. Of all places the stage is one of economies in effect, the moment is brief and such a fault as this is serious, practically.

In the Narrator's opening speech Mr. Williams has provided an excuse for music by saying that the play all happens in the memory, and memory always seems to move in music. That idea, or motif, goes well back to the classics: Phoebus replied and touched my trembling ear is Milton, but that in turn was Horace—*aurem vellit*—for the ear was the seat of memory. For *The Glass Menagerie*, therefore, Mr. Paul Bowles has written music that runs in and out of the scenes, sometimes, for a long interval, sometimes less. It seems to be a special gift of his, this writing music for a play that becomes a part of the play, strangely beautiful and strangely right.

Review of the 1956 Revival
of *The Glass Menagerie*

Brooks Atkinson

After eleven years Tennessee Williams' *The Glass Menagerie* has lost none of its wistful beauty. It was put on at the City Center last evening with Helen Hayes at the head of a sensitive performance.

In 1945 *The Glass Menagerie* established Mr. Williams as a practical dramatist. To see it again is to realize how much he has changed. There is a streak of savagery in his work now. The humor is bitter. The ugliness is shocking. He has come a long way since 1945—growing in mastery of the theatre, developing power, widening in scope. He has also renounced the tenderness that makes *The Glass Menagerie* such a delicate and moving play.

Probably he was closer to the characters of *The Glass Menagerie* than he has been to those of his later plays. For this is an idyl of St. Louis, where once he lived. There must be overtones of his own life in this tale of a dingy alley, shrouded down in poverty and despair. It is a perfect blend of humor and pathos, making a kind of sad poetry that is lovely, touching and a little grotesque. Mr. Williams has never improved on the daintiness and the shy allusiveness of the prose writing in this introductory play.

Everyone remembers with gratitude the acting of Laurette Taylor, Julie Haydon, Eddie Dowling and Anthony Ross in the original performance. Now we can be grateful for another beautiful rendering, under the direction of Alan Schneider. Although Miss Hayes has played the querulous and crochety mother in London, this is her first appearance in the part here. It is one of her finest. For Miss Hayes is the mistress of the little details as well as the broad outlines of a character, and she has brought them all to that enormous City Center stage—the fussiness, the pettiness, the silly coquetry as well as the desperate gallantry and the warmth of a mother trying to save her home.

Lois Smith plays the crippled, withdrawn daughter beautifully and poignantly. As the son James Daly is excellent—irritable and forgiving by turns, and fluent in his transitions from his duties as commentator to those of a pivotal character in the play. In the part of the gentleman caller, Lonny Chapman is admirable. Under the cheapness of this poseur, there is a solid fund of sympathy and understanding.

There is no doubt that the vast spaces of the City Center are unkind to the nuances of this requiem to two obscure women. *The Glass Menagerie* is really not quite so comic as it seems to be occasionally. But Miss Hayes and her associates understand it, respect it and weave around it the fabric of somber poetry. Although Mr. Williams has written some overwhelming dramas since 1945, he has not written anything so delicate and perceptive. *The Glass Menagerie* inhabits a half-world between comedy and tragedy where some wounding and amusing things occur.

Review of the 1965 Revival
of *The Glass Menagerie*

Howard Taubman

The durability of *The Glass Menagerie* is substantiated once again in the admirable revival at the Brooks Atkinson Theater. Tennessee Williams's first success stands up impressively 20 years after its introduction to New York. Of its four characters, all caught with sympathy and honesty, the most compelling remains Amanda.

Amanda's indestructibility is astonishing. If you first encountered her two decades ago in the magical performance of Laurette Taylor, you probably thought, as I did, that no one would ever dare the role again. Who could approach Miss Taylor? Had she not done more for Amanda through the alchemy of her art than the author?

In the intervening years I have seen a number of Amandas in productions scattered across the land, and I know now that Mr. Williams's Amanda, indeed Amanda herself, endures. She's credible, she is true. She is specifically American, and her truth transcends national traits.

Her essential lineaments remain fixed. She still clings stubbornly to memories and appearances of unforgotten elegance and irretrievable social glamour. Yet she does not really delude herself, for she faces up to the bitter reality of her situation. She fights to sustain her pride but can drain the sour cup of humiliation. She is fussy and meddlesome, shrewd and sharp-tongued, presumptuous and sensitive, embarrassing and infuriating, funny and pathetic. She is, in short, an indomitable creation.

No matter how different actresses of divergent gifts and temperaments recreate Amanda in their own images, the essential woman prevails. No matter how one or another trait is stressed or predominates in any performance, the powerful leverage of the character remains. Could there be more convincing proof of how truly Mr. Williams wrought?

Memories

But a role in a drama to an actor, like the notes in a symphonic score to a conductor, is the basic source material, not the finished product. The speeches and instructions provided by the playwright, however precise, are the potter's clay. The task of shaping remains for the actor, guided by the director. Different tastes and intuitions can produce marked differentiations in a character.

Recalling a number of Amandas, I am struck by the diversity she has assumed. From Miss Taylor, the first, to Maureen Stapleton, the latest, each Amanda has been not only the mother of Mr. Williams's imagining but also uniquely individualized. Each interpretation has found new lights and shadows in the role; each has made subtle distinctions in the play.

Miss Taylor, more than any Amanda I remember, bathed the character in the muted glow of lost, aching illusions. No one has ever matched her in evoking a sense of the faded past. She did not merely cloak herself in a remembrance of vanished gentility. It shone from her in a kind of brave, though dimming radiance. She did not need to adorn herself in her old-fashioned party dress to conjure up the fond, foolish atmosphere of a happy girlhood in a graceful, magnolia-scented South. The inflections of her speech, her looks, her gestures and movements created mood as well as character.

Underneath the airs and pretensions of Miss Taylor's Amanda, there was the necessary and irreducible core of fierce determination. Her fussing over her son, Tom, was a compulsive habit. Her sentimentality about her daughter, Laura, and her nostalgia for her own youth as a Southern belle were self-indulgences of which she was aware. She might pretend to helplessness and hope to appeal to gallantry as of yore, but she left no doubt that she would seek to command the situation.

You believed with all your heart that her claim to social refinements was not vain-glory. This Amanda had once been what she said she was. The charm she wore so readily was an old accomplishment, and the swiftness with which she assumed it in a trying or painful moment was a perfect reflection of what one remembered of gracious, calculating Southern ladies one had known.

Some years later I saw the Amanda of another famous actress. A familiarity with Southern coquetry was in this performance as well as a grasp of the woman's basic toughness. But these elements had not been fused into a cohesive interpretation. There was too much effort to emphasize the amusing contradictions in Amanda. One felt after a while that the role was being played too hard for laughs, as if the performer unknowingly was mocking Amanda.

The effect on the balance of the play as a whole was not salutary. Yet the essential brooding atmosphere was not forfeited completely. Somehow Amanda survived the misinterpretation. The halflights of *The Glass Menagerie,* though distorted, cast their haunting spell.

A third actress made more of the iron in Amanda's will than any other player I had seen. The laughter implicit in her was almost suppressed, replaced by implacable rigidity and drive. The reasons for Tom's urge to escape and for Laura's pathological need for self-effacement were cruelly transparent. Again the balance was wrong. Nevertheless, Amanda had force.

This Amanda

Miss Stapleton brings probing values of her own to Amanda. The womanliness and motherliness take on a new significance. The spirit of Southern gentility is not noticeable. The troubling sense of genteel decay is there, though the geography is not distinctly identified. The laughter is tinged by despair. A strain of tenderness runs through the woman. She is divertingly and sadly domineering, but not monstrously.

She is still Amanda, the pivot of the family. But because this is an Amanda of subtly different facture, the relationships around her fall into new textures. Thus the nature and caliber of actors modify the fabric of a play.

It no longer is any secret that in the original cast there were hidden hostilities between Miss Taylor and Eddie Dowling, who played Tom, and the result was a brittleness and antagonism between mother and son. Miss Stapleton and George Grizzard do not conceal the abrasiveness, but one never doubts their mutual affection.

Pat Hingle's splendidly decent and commonplace Gentleman Caller confers a fresh significance on the long, affecting scene with Piper Laurie's Laura. Here is another vivid example of the special illumination a gifted actor can bring to a familiar role. The play takes on new strength from his insights.

The Film Version
of *The Glass Menagerie* (1950)

Maurice Yacowar

The first Tennessee Williams film can serve as a textbook demonstration of how insensitive compromises can ruin an adaptation. Williams conceived *The Glass Menagerie* in a nonnaturalistic mode, with expressionistic lighting and music and with a filmic flow of short scenes. But filmic elements in a theatrical production may not work the same way when used in a film; for one thing, the surprise is gone. Perhaps an extremely theatrical device might be necessary in a film, for equivalence to a filmic device on stage. In any case, Williams seemed to forestall any filming of the play, when he cited in his production notes "the unimportance of the photographic in art." Reality is "an organic thing which the poetic imagination can represent, or suggest, in essence, only through transformation" (p ix). The scene, we are told, is memory and therefore unrealistic, omitting some details and emphasizing others, "according to the emotional value" of the material, for "memory is seated predominantly in the heart" (p. 3). But film is seated predominantly in the physical reality. In the film of *The Glass Menagerie,* the poetic spirit of the original is sacrificed to the literal realism of a conventional romantic film.

In the play, Laura Wingfield is a shy, crippled girl who collects glass animals as a refuge from the demands and shocks of the outside world. Her mother Amanda is a vain Southern belle who hoards fantasies of success and nags her children until they try to escape her—Laura to her menagerie, son Tom to the life of a wandering sailor. Tom seems modeled after Williams himself, an aspiring poet who works in a shoe warehouse and finally flees his family. The action centers around the dinner visit of Jim O'Connor, Tom's friend from work, whom Amanda takes to be a possible suitor for Laura. But Jim is engaged. The evening ends with Amanda's hopes dashed and Laura's favorite glass piece, a unicorn, with its horn broken off, now just an ordinary horse.

The primary failure of the film was the producers' insistence upon a happy ending.[1] Where the play dramatized the impossibility of achieving one's dreams (Amanda, Jim) or of escaping one's limits either physical (Laura) or emotional (Tom), the film affirms the shallow confidence of O'Connor. Laura is not left lonely and abandoned, as in the play; instead, we last see her as a happy, well-adjusted girl, coolly awaiting her own gentleman caller.

Consistent with this recovery, Laura is normalized throughout the film. In the play she was pathologically shy, too shy even to go to her typing class. In the film she bravely goes to class but is—justifiably—repelled by a cruel teacher and an excessively difficult exam. Thus Williams's hypersensitive creature is transformed into a patient, reasonable girl who is offended beyond endurance.

Director Irving Rapper altered the material to enhance Laura's normalcy. For example, in Williams's opening scene, Amanda confronts Laura with her truancy and lying. But this scene does not occur until the middle of the film. Williams's powerful scene of character revelation is thus reduced to trivial suspense over whether or not Laura will be caught in her truancy. Moreover, the footage of Laura's visits to the zoo suggests that she is enjoying herself, not that she is wandering lonely and homeless, as in the play.

The film diminishes the imaginative hold that Laura has on Tom, by making her seem just a normal girl. In the play, Tom remains haunted by Laura's memory. He feels guilty for having abandoned her. But in the film Laura gently sends Tom off on his way; she can manage without him. In the play, Tom's recollection was forced by the strength of Laura's presence in his mind. In the film, Tom begins by complaining about the boredom of a sailor on dog watch. From idleness, not from obsession, does his mind turn to his Laura.

Actually, the film reduces the complexity of all the major characters. Amanda loses honor and her aristocratic unworldliness when the film shows her quarreling over an unpaid bill in a department store. Similarly, Tom's dreams of adventure are reduced to an exotic lie told to confuse a pick-up in a bar. But, with the exception of Laura, the worst casualty is Jim O'Connor. In the play, Jim is a subtle example of failure, the high-school hero who sustains his optimism despite his failure to realize his promise. Williams presents him as a charming, simple fellow. But in the film, Jim is played as a hero. He glibly maneuvers his foreman and colleagues. Gone is his veneration of the inventor of chewing gum! The only trace of irony in O'Connor's character in the film is the fact that his longest chat with Tom occurs in the men's washroom. The irony fails because the scene still suggests that the figure is superior to his surroundings, not—as in the play—subdued by them.

The film also omits Jim's double service as Romantic Dream and—as Tom introduces him—as "the most realistic character in the play, being an emissary from a world of reality that we were somehow set apart from" (p. 5). First, the Romance. In the play, Laura first mentions Jim to Amanda as a boy she admired in high school. For one shocking moment, then, his appearance seems to be the miraculous fulfillment of her dreams. This makes her ultimate disappointment all the greater. The film omits the confiding in Amanda, so Laura's involvement with Jim is simplified.

Nor does Jim serve as an "emissary from reality," because the film shows the Wingfield family in the outside world of reality. Laura is at home in the zoo, Amanda in the stores, and Tom in the streets and bars. By opening out the action, the film dissipates the play's sense of oppressive confinement in the Wingfield apartment. Irving Rapper actually reverses the values of the play when he has Jim step in from the rain (a trademark of Rapper's films), thereby suggesting that the Wingfield apartment is a comfortable haven. It is not. In this instance the "freedom" of the camera violated the play's tension for escape.

Other, minor insensitivities abound in the film. Laura is shown buying her unicorn en route to her typing class. In the play she had treasured that piece for thirteen years. Again, the film simplifies Laura's emotion. The broken unicorn is no longer Laura's long-time favorite, indeed her emblem; it is just a piece of glass. In the play Jim whirls Laura around for a short dance in the living room, causing the unicorn to break, while in the film the dance is made public, at the hall across the alley. The film here disrupts the delicate balance between privacy and exposure in Williams's scene.

Rapper also violates the consistency of Tom's perspective upon the action. Often the film shows us what Tom did not see, and so could not remember in a memory play. Amanda's memory of her success with seventeen gentleman callers at a ball is the most striking example. Firstly, Rapper shows the scene as an event, not as a story, so he eliminates the possibility that the tale is Amanda's invention. Secondly, we see it as a part of what Tom sees or experiences throughout the film, although the scene is Amanda's memory, not Tom's. Finally, Rapper's Amanda kisses a number of the men, a detail in conflict with Amanda's pretense to romantic gentility. Similarly, the subjective shot of Laura limping loudly to her desk is outside Tom's experience; it is a striking effect but it disturbs the logic of the drama.

In addition to these minor difficulties, the film fails to develop an equivalent for the poetic techniques of the play. For example, in the play the expressionistic lighting of Laura suggests her apartness from the others, even a luminosity in her spirit. In the film Laura is lit naturalistically, so her character loses much of its poetic effect. Similarly, the portrait of Tom's father lights up from time to time in the play, again expressing the strong character of the man who fled the family and who remains a lively example to Tom. When the father figures in the conversation or thought of the film, Rapper provides the traditional close-up or keeps the picture in focus behind the characters. The general effect is the same: the portrait is emphasized. But replacing a surprising stage effect with a familiar film device produces a less exciting style (and in this case reduces the strength of the father's image).

Only once does the film reach for the expressionistic lighting of the play. When Jim leaves the Wingfields, a whitewall tire in front of the alley flashes on and off, catching the lights from the dance hall. This is a clever shot but it fails in logic: the image of tempting mobility should be associated with Tom's escape, not Jim's. And the devices of luminous representation should be associated with Laura and the father, as in the play, not with a tire on a stranger's car.

In addition to these failures in script and in filming, the cast of big names did not meet the artistic needs of the play. Laura's fragility and delicacy are lost in the vigor, solidity, and discretion that characterized Jane Wyman's persona as The Indomitable Sufferer from *Johnny Belinda* (1948) on. Gertrude Lawrence was a compromise casting—Rapper wanted Tallulah Bankhead—and she proved too earthy for Amanda, too ready with wink or haggard grimace. The role of faded Southern flower was not within Lawrence's easy range, and the script and Rapper's direction rendered it remoter still. Thus, the film makes Amanda even more strident than the play ("You're not crippled! Walk, Laura. . . . I want to see you walk!"). The development of Laura's relationship with Jim is continually interrupted by shots of Amanda mugging at Tom. Finally, Kirk Douglas performs well as Jim, but his persona is too hearty, energetic, likable, and affluent to express the sham success of Williams's O'Connor. The play's simple failure becomes in the film a hero of substance and style.

By providing this simple "hero" and by giving Laura a happy romantic ending, the film relates to the original play—as the horse does to the unicorn. Something distinctive and extremely personal has been converted into something simple and prosaic, the standard romantic melodrama. Williams rightly declares it "the most awful travesty of the play I've ever seen. . . horribly mangled by the people who did the film-script."[2]

Notes

[1]Hugh MacMullan, "Translating *The Glass Menagerie* to Film," *Hollywood Quarterly*, V (1950–51), pp. 14–32.

[2]John Calendo, "Tennessee Talks to John Calendo," *Interview*, April 1973, p. 44.

Menagerie, Glass and Wine:
Tennessee Williams and Hart Crane

Gilbert Debusscher

Although talkative and candid about his private life, Tennessee Williams has always been reticent about his work. He has in fact expressed strong feelings about the need for secrecy in order to protect "a thing that depends on seclusion till its completion for its safety."[1] However, he has repeatedly over the years mentioned other writers who have deeply influenced him. When pressed for names he never fails to mention Hart Crane, D. H. Lawrence, and Anton Chekhov. The influence of Lawrence and Chekhov has been examined extensively, but that of Hart Crane has largely been neglected.

Yet the external evidence of Crane's importance to Williams is overwhelming. First introduced to the slim volume of Crane's *Collected Poems* by Clark Mills McBurney, a poet whom he had befriended in St. Louis in 1935, Williams himself later acknowledged his debt in the "Frivolous Version" of his "Preface to My Poems": "It was Clark who warned me of the existence of people like Hart Crane and Rimbaud and Rilke, and (. . .) removed my attention from the more obvious to the purer voices in poetry. About this time I acquired my copy of Hart Crane's collected poems which I began to read with gradual comprehension."[2]

In this early mention Williams already reserves a special place for Crane, associating him—as he will throughout his career—with "the purer voices in poetry."

Shortly after coming into possession of the *Poems,* Williams further acquired a portrait of his favorite poet from a book in the Jacksonville Public Library. He had it framed and has taken it with him, along with the poems, wherever his bohemian life has led him. Out of the sixteen allusions to Hart Crane in the *Letters to Donald Windham,* three are to that treasured portrait.[3]

Besides these two tangible reminders of Crane in Williams's surroundings, clear traces of the poet's presence can be found in the plays. In *You Touched Me!,* the dramatization of a D. H. Lawrence story which Williams wrote in collaboration with Donald Windham in the early forties, there is already an explicit reference to Crane.[4] In 1947 Williams borrowed the fifth stanza of Crane's poem "The Broken Tower" as a motto for *A Streetcar Named Desire*[5] and in the following year, 1948, the playwright published *Summer and Smoke,* the title of which came from Crane's "Emblems of Conduct."[6]

In following years, Williams mentions Crane in correspondence less often than before. In fact, only in 1959, with the publication of *Sweet Bird of Youth,* does Crane regain his former prominence. The motto of the play comes from Crane's *White Buildings* collection, appearing in the piece entitled "Legend."[7] In 1962, in *The Night of the Iguana,* Williams again alludes to Crane, but rather than to the poetry, the reference is now to the portrait of the poet painted in 1931 by the Mexican artist David Siqueiros.[8]

Williams's continued preoccupation with the poet culminated in 1965, when he agreed to read a selection of poems by Crane for Caedmon Records and to provide a note for the slipcover.[9] In the note Williams reveals his familiarity with the facts of Crane's life and mentions two early scholarly works devoted to the poet: the "superb" biography written by Philip Horton (1937), and the "marvelous" collection of letters edited by Brom Weber (1952). The particular incidents on which Williams concentrates illustrate themes and motifs basic to his own creative work. He focuses with dramatic flair on the most intense moments of Crane's life, the day of his suicide and the emotionally charged night immediately preceding it. Of the latter, we are told that Crane "had visited the sailors' quarters and the visit had turned out badly—they had treated him mockingly and violently." Regarding the day itself, Williams describes how Peggy Cowley, the woman with whom Crane was traveling back to the United States, "had . . . suffered, that same night before, the pointless accident of a book of matches blowing up in her hand and burning her hand severely. She was not in a state to sympathize much with her friend, and so what happened happened."

Crane's confrontation with the outside world is here presented as similar to that of many of the more sensitive characters in Williams's work—particularly the artists and the poets. Wherever they turn in their search for understanding or togetherness, in their quest for "the visionary company of love," they meet with rejection, hostility or indifference. The note further mentions the writing block Crane experienced in the last two years of his life, after adverse criticism of *The Bridge* had reawakened self-doubt:

> Crane had lived with such fearful intensity—and without fearful intensity Crane was unable to work at all—that his nerves were exhausted and for many months he had been able to produce only one important poem, *The Broken Tower,* a poem that contains these beautiful and ominous lines:

> The bells, I say, the bells
> Break down their tower.[10]

"By the bells breaking down their tower," Williams goes on to say, Crane "undoubtedly meant the romantic and lyric intensity of his vocation." That Williams considers the lines "ominous" indicates that he views the creative process here, as elsewhere in his own work, as a consuming experience.[11] The production of poetry and, more generally, of art leaves the artist ultimately exhausted, spent as a runner and broken in body. One cannot help noting the parallel with Williams's own career, which went into a prolonged eclipse in the early 1960s—at the time he recorded the Crane poems—when he doggedly rewrote *The Milktrain Doesn't Stop Here Anymore* and relied more and more heavily on alcohol and drugs to alleviate doubts about his artistic future. His remarks about Crane's state of mind could therefore apply equally to himself: "He lived in a constant inner turmoil and storm that liquor, which he drank recklessly, was no longer able to quieten, to hold in check".

Finally the Caedmon note contains a quotation that points to one of the elements of Crane's life that fascinated Williams. The short passage from "For the Marriage of Faustus and Helen" (erroneously identified by Williams as belonging to "The Broken Tower") reads: "There is the world dimensional for those untwisted by the love of things irreconcilable" (*Poems,* p. 98). Williams interprets these lines as follows: "The meaning . . . is more open to varying interpretations. Could he have meant that his vocation as a poet of extraordinary purity, as well as intensity, was hopelessly at odds with his nighttime search for love in waterfront bars?" The Williams of the *Memoirs* is here clearly identifying with one aspect of Crane's personality which he sees in the cryptic lines.[12]

The record note, then, although devoted to Crane, reveals beyond the rapidly sketched portrait of the poet a figure in the carpet that closely resembles Williams's own face and that of all the poet-characters in whom he had projected himself up to 1965. It strongly suggests, further, that if Hart Crane enduringly captured Williams's imagination, the cause was biographical as well as poetic. Williams was aware, as he later stated in an interview with Cecil Brown,[13] of the truly stunning similarity of his and Crane's formative years, family situations, and aspirations. Crane's small-town origins; his family life, torn between egotistical parents who turned him into the battlefield of their marital dissentions; his fervent attachment to both his neurotic mother and his indulgent, doting grandmother; his early aversion to and later reconciliation with a father who opposed his aspirations as a poet and insisted that he enter the family business; the Bohemian wanderlust that prevented his settling down permanently;[14] his bouts of ill health, which were often psychosomatic in origin; and finally, his uphill fight for artistic integrity in an uncomprehending world, tormented by spells of self-doubt and despair that led him to suicide—all of these, together with a sexuality unfocused but predominantly homoerotic, were traits of Crane's life and personality in which Williams must have recognized himself as in a mirror. I submit, therefore, that Hart Crane contributed forcefully to Williams's perception of himself as revealed by the semi-autobiographical characters which populate his plays, the figure of the wandering poet, the doomed artist who haunts the published work, appearing as early as *Battle of Angels* (1938)—a figure which finds its most surprising incarnation in Tom Wingfield in *The Glass Menagerie* (1944).

The Glass Menagerie belongs to a period of Williams's highest involvement with the poetry of Hart Crane. But at first sight Crane appears to be totally absent from this particular play. I would suggest that Crane is indeed present in *The Glass Menagerie,* but that it is only the mode of his presence which is here different. Whereas in *A Streetcar Named Desire* and *Summer and Smoke* he is emphatically visible through motto or title, in this play he pervades the texture of the play without being explicitly mentioned.

There is nevertheless one objective clue (perhaps even two, as I will show) that attests to Williams's use of Crane. When Amanda appears in her "resurrected" yellow dress for the "jonquil scene", in Scene Six, Williams describes the special quality of this moment of great intensity through a stage direction which reads: "the legend of her youth is nearly revived."[15] Recall again the passage from Crane's poem "Legend" which serves as motto for *Sweet Bird of Youth.* This stage direction is a clear hint for the reader and the director aware of the Crane–Williams crosscurrents that Amanda, in her pathetic attempt to recapture her past glory, is to experience the disillusionment of those who force themselves into "relentless capers," ceaselessly reliving their past. The borrowing further confirms that the Southern background that Amanda recollects is in fact a "legend," that is, both a key to an understanding of her character and motivations and a story, a fable, perhaps a lie. It suggests that the past was never as idyllic as she wants to remember it as being, but at the same time—to those who are aware of Crane's poem, and beyond it, of John Donne's "The Canonization"—[16]it indicates that this is a cautionary tale for all those who must turn their backs on their youthful past and move forward to maturity and decline. The borrowing relegated to a stage direction is a faint reminder at this crucial moment that Amanda's fate is meant to be a model, a "legend" to be considered and learned from.

A more cryptic reminder of Crane may be found later in the same scene, again in a stage direction. In the course of a conversation with Jim, Tom rhapsodically describes a future that involves neither his mother, his sister, nor the shoe factory. As the image of "the sailing vessel with the Jolly Roger again" is projected on a screen in the background, Tom leans over the rail of the fire escape on which he stands, now become the rail of an imaginary ocean liner, and the stage direction reads: "He looks like a voyager" (p. 201). The precise term for one who travels by sea cannot fail, for someone familiar (as Tennessee Williams is) with the Crane canon, to evoke the "Voyages" poems. Indeed the word so fittingly limns Hart Crane that John Unterecker entitled his monumental 1969 biography of the poet *Voyager: A Life of Hart Crane.*

The short scene in which Tom leans on the rail may be a dramatic reconstitution of the last minutes of the poet's life before he escaped, as Tom is planning to do, from a world that had become too oppressive to bear. What we may have, then, is a shadowy portrait in

Tom Wingfield of Hart Crane himself, at a most critical moment in his life. Just as Williams's own face could be glimpsed behind his portrait of Crane in the record note, so the figure of Crane shows through Tom Wingfield's portrait in *The Glass Menagerie,* providing it with tantalizing shadows.

Moreover, although there is by now a long tradition, supported by declarations of the playwright himself, that the figure of Amanda Wingfield is a portrait of Williams's own mother, one could make a convincing case for Grace Hart Crane, the poet's mother, as the model for some aspects of the high-strung, possessive Amanda. One should recall, in this connection, the anecdote of Mrs. Williams's visit to Chicago for a performance of *The Glass Menagerie,* at the end of which she was appalled to hear that Laurette Taylor may have considered her the real-life model for the character she portrayed in the play. Furthermore, a growing number of commentators have noticed, again following the playwright's indications, that the play is hardly a faithful picture of the Williamses' circumstances around 1935–36, and that the three characters supposedly modeled on the author and his family have all undergone important changes in the process of dramatization.

If one remembers, on the other hand, the picture of Hart Crane's mother as it emerges from the accounts of Philip Horton and John Unterecker, one realizes not only that the relationships of the sons with their respective mothers are comparable, but that the two women show a remarkable degree of resemblance even in details. For example, Mrs. Crane, suddenly deprived of the financial security that had thus far seemed assured, contemplates taking a job "as hostess in a restaurant, perhaps assistant in one of the city's hotels, anything that would let her draw on the only assets she had—her charm and her beauty".[17] Of this, more than an echo can be found in the job Amanda holds, being a more practical-minded woman, "at Famous Barr . . . demonstrating those (she indicates a brassiere with her hands)" (*Glass Menagerie,* p. 154). In Williams's conception, the job—which his own mother never had to contemplate—capitalized on Amanda's physical appeal; one of the early drafts sent to Audrey Wood read: "Amanda has been working as a model for matrons' dresses at downtown department store and has just lost the job because of faded appearance."[18]

The picture of Mrs. Crane painted by Unterecker in the following paragraph is exactly like Amanda, with her reminiscences about the carefree Blue Mountain girl courted by seventeen gentleman callers: "As she and Hart would talk through her problems, both of them would look back fondly to Hart's childhood, to the days when financial security seemed limitless—the good times of gardeners, maids, cooks, chauffeurs, handymen, tutors—until, magnifying the past out of all proportion, they would make the present unbearable."[19]

These glimpses of Grace Crane cohere into a prototype for Amanda as plausible as the playwright's own mother. But the resemblance between Mrs. Crane and Amanda is never more convincing than in the following passage: "For Grace's real problem—and to a considerable extent, Hart's—was the memory of former affluence. . . . Each of them found it easier to eat badly than to dress badly. Keeping up appearances was for Grace not just a casual compulsion but a life-and-death matter."[20] Such a portrait anticipates Amanda's D.A.R. outfit, her compulsive refurbishing of the apartment, the purchase of new clothes for Laura, her metamorphosis into a Southern belle in her own "resurrected" dress, and her evocation of the past for the benefit of the bewildered Jim O'Connor.

Let me now advance a further argument: beyond these strong biographical parallels with Crane and his mother, the play also reflects the influence of Crane as a poet and of one poem particularly, *viz*—"The Wine Menagerie," from the collection *White Buildings*. To begin with, there is the striking similarity of the titles. The present title of the play was arrived at only after various other possibilities such as "Portrait of a Girl in Glass," "The Gentleman Caller," and "If You Breathe It Breaks or Portrait of a Girl in Glass" had been discarded.[21] I therefore suggest that it is only after growing aware of the correspondences between his play and Crane's poem, presumably late in the process of fashioning the final version, that Williams hit upon this felicitous title for the play that was to establish his reputation throughout the world. It is my guess that at some point during the rehearsals—perhaps well into December 1944, when Eddie Dowling and George Jean Nathan advised him to introduce the drunk scene finally included at the beginning of Scene Six[22]—Williams was reminded of "The Wine Menagerie," and used this as the spark for his final title. The first two lines of the poem in fact could have served as a reasonable starting frame for the whole scene:

> Invariably when the wine redeems the sight
> Narrowing the mustard scansions of the eyes . . . (*Poems*, p. 92)

Regarding these lines, R. W. B. Lewis comments that "the consumption of much wine . . . suddenly clarified the poet's vision and greatly increased his interpretive and creative powers."[23] Tom's drunkenness in the play is a source of similar vision. In his conversation with Laura, Tom presents the stage show he has just seen—an escape act by a music hall magician—in terms that leave little doubt of its symbolic connection with his own fate. Through his report we come to realize that escaping the social and emotional web in which he is entangled without hurting anyone and hence without feeling guilty is a trick that only a magician could bring off. This truth revealed in drunkenness helps justify Tom's final action in the play and helps make the audience accept the fact that "to escape from a trap he has to act without pity." (*Glass Menagerie,* p. 123).

The second stanza of the poem introduces the idea that the whole piece should be seen as the intoxicated musing—"a boozy approximation of direct statement"[24]—of the poet, who also figures as a character in the bar scene which the lines evoke. This double role as writer and character is paralleled in the play, where Tom is both the narrator and a character in the story he tells. Moreover, several Crane commentators have noticed that—like the play—"The Wine Menagerie" supports a reading in terms of the poet's biography.[25] And there are further similarities: Crane's poem suggests, as Sherman Paul has emphasized, that "the man and woman, whose combat [the narrator-actor] witnesses . . . are father and mother seen from the 'distance' of childhood."[26] This is essentially the point of view of Tom, whose "distance in time" (*Glass Menagerie,* p. 236) provides him with a perspective akin to although not identical with that of the poet in Crane's work.[27] The seasonal setting and atmosphere of the two works present additional affinities. The bleak early winter landscape of the poem, which contributes to the Eliotian atmosphere of the whole, is traceable also in the general mood of the play. It informs the urban setting common to play and poem and presides over the description of "the couples . . . in the alley . . . kissing behind ash pits and telephone poles" (*Glass Menagerie,* p. 179), who could have been lifted by Williams from the context Crane had earlier devised for them.

Thematically, too, the poem offers a basis for comparison with the play. Uncharacteristically for Crane, "loss is the primary emotion the poem reaches into."[28] Now "loss" is a key concept in

Williams's vision, a feeling that he finds inseparable from the human condition. "The monosyllable of the clock is loss, loss, loss, unless you devote your heart to its opposition," he has said.[29] Surveying the isolation of the derelict "menagerie" assembled in the bar, Crane's poem ends in sadness, or—as Paul has aptly put it—on "a low plateau of resolve."[30] This again is a perfect description of the final moment of *The Glass Menagerie:* the mood of melancholy and nostalgia suffusing the play may, then, owe as much to Hart Crane as to Anton Chekhov, who has long been thought its primary source.

The nostalgia at the end of the play is poignantly enhanced by Tom's ultimate departure, by his painful act of tearing himself away from his family and the guilt associated with this emotional and physical exile. Tom's basic motivation and his final summoning up courage are clearly foreshadowed in the poem, where the young man is exhorted to

> Rise from the dates and crumbs. And walk away . . .
> Beyond the wall . . .
> And fold your exile on your back again . . . (*Poems,* p. 94)

Both characters come in the end to accept that freedom and its corollary, loneliness, are essential to the creative activity which they see as their ultimate reason to live.

The situation of Tom in the epilogue may have been suggested by that of the speaker in the poem, a solitary man in a bar looking at a display of multicolored bottles in which are reflected the movements and attitudes of patrons, images encompassing the past as much as the present. Peering in drunken fascination at the changing surfaces of the "glozening decanters," the poet manages to focus on essentials, "narrowing the mustard scansions of the eyes." He thus sees through or beyond the chaotic reality that otherwise claims his attention and, through vision, imposes an order on it—"asserts a vision in the slumbering gaze" (*Poems,* p. 92).

Tom looks not at bottles on display in a bar, but at delicately colored vials in the window of a perfume shop. They too present an informal, unpatterned reality, "like bits of a shattered rainbow" (*Glass Menagerie,* p. 237). They reflect, far beyond the drab winter of the city, the past of Tom's family life, "conscript(ing)" him (to use Crane's word) to the shadowy glow of the menagerie.[31] In Williams's case, the play itself is the vision that imposes order and exorcises—if only temporarily—the conflicting feelings of relief and guilt stirred in Tom by memory.

Finally, poem and play have a further point of confluence. Crane's poem establishes a number of mythic parallels for its central incident, a confrontation between a man and a woman in a bar. Evoking the violent meetings of Judith and Holofernes, Salome and John the Baptist, and Petrushka and his "valentine," it presents the experience as one of dismemberment and decapitation. The figurine central to the glass collection, the unicorn, undergoes a comparable mutilation when its little horn is accidentally broken off. This interpretation is particularly apt if one remembers that the glass animal represents Rose, the playwright's sister, and that the loss of the horn is probably an attenuated echo of the prefrontal lobotomy—a modern surgical version of decapitation—which alleviated her schizophrenia but left her maimed for life.

Both poem and play, then, can rightfully be seen as "an actual incident, in a clear setting, with visible characters and progressing from a meandering meditation to a moment of clear decision, a decision, needless to say, about the exercise of the poet's visionary power and touching upon his creative resolve."[32] Rather than an indulgent wallowing in sentimental reminiscences, *The Glass Menagerie* may be viewed through a Cranean glass, as a dramatic statement about the artist and his predicament. This may lead to a further conclusion, again constituting a warning for all who would limit the play to a faithful account of Williams's early days in St. Louis, that *The Glass Menagerie* is literature as much as confession, imaginative reading as much as autobiography, Crane as much as Williams.

Notes

[1]Henry Hewes, "American Playwrights Self-Appraised," *Saturday Review,* Sept. 3, 1955, p. 18. The best gathering and piecing together of available evidence on Williams's artistic practice is to be found in William J. Miller's *Modern Playwrights at Work* (New York, 1968), I, 375–85. See also Marvin Spivack, "Tennessee Williams: The Idea of the Theater," *Jahrbuch für Amerikastudien* 10 (1965): 221–31.

[2]Reprinted in *Where I Live: Selected Essays by Tennessee Williams,* ed. Christine R. Day and Bob Woods (New York: New Directions, 1978), p. 3.

[3]*Tennessee Williams's Letters to Donald Windham, 1940–1965,* ed. Donald Windham (New York: Holt, Rinehart, and Winston, 1977). It is interesting to note, for what statistics are worth, that Crane is the writer most frequently mentioned in this collection; Lawrence is mentioned thirteen times, Chekhov eight times.

⁴Tennessee Williams and Donald Windham, *You Touched Me! A Romantic Comedy in Three Acts.* (New York: Samuel French, 1947) Copyrighted in 1942 and 1947, the play was first produced in September 1945. When Hadrian reads at random from Matilda's book of verse he comes across the lines

> "How like a caravan my heart—
> Across the desert moved towards yours!"

and wonders "Toward whose? Who is this H. C. it's dedicated to?" to which Matilda shyly replies "Hart Crane. An American poet who died ten years ago." Besides the explicit reference, the two lines read by Hadrian recall the "speechless caravan" in the fifth stanza of "To Brooklyn Bridge," the piece with which Crane's epic of America opens. [*The Complete Poems of Hart Crane,* ed. Waldo Frank (New York, 1958) p. 3: Quotations of the poetry throughout are from this edition.]

5   And so it was I entered the broken world
           To trace the visionary company of love, its voice
           An instant in the wind (I know not whither hurled)
           But not for long to hold each desperate choice.
>   *Poems,* pp. 139–40

⁶The alliterative phrase appears in the only two lines—the first two of the three quoted below—that are Crane's own, inserted between fragments gleaned in the then unpublished manuscripts of Samuel Greenberg

> By that time summer and smoke were past.
> Dolphins still played, arching the horizons,
> But only to build memories of spiritual gates.
>   *Poems,* p. 68

7   Relentless caper for all those who step
           The legend of their youth into the noon.
>   *Poems,* p. 66

⁸The reference appears in Act II in the dialogue between Shannon and Hannah, a painter who is also the play's psychoanalyst. She is trying to sketch a picture not so much of Shannon's outward appearance as of a deeper reality hidden within him:

> *Hannah:* . . . You're a very difficult subject. When the Mexican painter, Siqueiros did his portrait of the American poet Hart Crane he had to paint him with closed eyes because he couldn't paint his eyes open—there was too much suffering in them and he couldn't paint it.

The Theater of Tennessee Williams IV (New York: New Directions, 1972), p. 302.
⁹"Tennessee Williams Reads Hart Crane," TC 1206, 1965.
¹⁰In the original the two lines quoted by Williams form a single line.
¹¹For a fictional treatment of this view the reader should turn to Williams's neglected short story "The Poet," in the collection *One Arm* (1948). Almost contemporary with this short story—it is dated August 1949—is a little-known preface Williams wrote for Oliver Evans's *Young Man with a Screwdriver* (Lincoln: University of Nebraska Press, 1949). Evans's collection of poems contains a piece entitled "For Hart Crane" (p. 23) which deals with the circumstances of Crane's suicide at sea and ends with an allusion to Baudelaire's *L'Albatros* and its depiction of the poet alienated in a hostile world. In the preface Williams inevitably mentions

Crane and provides, by contrast with Evans, a definition *a contrario* of his favorite poem and a succinct view of what the short story presents in fiction form. "Although flashes of poetic genius are not absent from this volume, it is not of a tortured compulsive kind. Speaking of that demon, I think invariably of Hart Crane, at the very center of whose life it exploded, and destroyed. The dynamics of this work are, of course, less intense, but also more benign. It is illuminated without a sense of violence. The poet himself is not ravaged. He lives with his art instead of *by* or *for* it, which is happier for him and even somehow, more comforting for his listeners. The poetry contained in this volume is not of the explosive or compulsive kind, nor is it the work of a deliberately and self-consciously professional man of letters" (pp. 1-2).

[12]This is not the only instance in which Williams identifies with Crane. In the "Serious Version" Williams described the difficulties encountered by young artists, stating that he had known some who had found "the struggle too complex and exhausting to go on with." He adds, "Hart Crane wasn't the only one. I have lived in the middle of it since I was released from the comparative cocoon of schools and colleges" (*Where I Live,* eds. Day and Woods, p. 5). Moreover, the dichotomy established here between purity and sensual gratification reminds us of all the early heroines who are rent by the conflict between demanding sensuality and an aspiration toward the ideal. It is interesting in this respect to remember that Williams has repeatedly claimed, "I am Blanche Dubois."

[13]"Interview with Tennessee Williams," *Partisan Review* 45 (1978): 276–305.

[14]Nancy Tischler strongly emphasizes this aspect of Crane's appeal to Williams: "More than anything else, Hart Crane must have appealed to Williams on a purely personal level. He must have felt a kinship with this lonely, Dionysian poet—a homeless wanderer like himself" [*Tennessee Williams: Rebellious Puritan* (New York: The Citadel Press, 1961), p. 65.]

[15]*The Theatre of Tennessee Williams* I (New York: New Directions, 1971), p. 193. All quotations of the play are from this edition.

[16]R. W. B. Lewis, *The Poetry of Hart Crane* (Princeton: Princeton University Press, 1967), p. 139 n.

[17]John Unterecker, *Voyager: A Life of Hart Crane* (New York: Farrar, Strauss, and Giroux, 1969), p. 236. See also the account of the same period in Philip Horton, *Hart Crane: The Life of an American Poet* (New York: The Viking Press, 1937), pp. 117–18.

[18]The draft is reprinted in *The World of Tennessee Williams,* ed. Richard F. Leavitt (New York: G. P. Putnam's Sons, 1978), pp. 52–53.

[19]Unterecker, *Voyager,* p. 236.

[20]*Ibid.,* p. 533.

[21]It is surprising that *The Glass Menagerie* acquired its final title only a few months before its Chicago premiere. In the correspondence with Windham it is referred to repeatedly in 1943 and 1944, but always as "The Gentleman Caller" or "Caller" (*Letters,* pp. 59, 60, 94, 140, 148). Rehearsals began in December 1944, first in New York and then in Chicago, where the play opened on 26 December 1944 as *The Glass Menagerie.* Exactly when after 25 August 1944, the date of the last mention of the old title to Windham, the play acquired its definitive title is not, to the best of my knowledge, ascertainable.

[22]On this episode, see *Letters,* pp. 154–55.

[23]*Hart Crane,* p. 195.

[24]*Ibid.,* p. 193.

[25]See, among others, Herbert A. Leibowitz, *Hart Crane: An Introduction to the Poetry* (New York: Columbia University Press, 1968), pp. 3–4; and Paul, *Hart's Bridge,* p. 128.

[26]*Hart's Bridge,* p. 123.

[27]The short story\version clearly establishes that Tom is reminiscing about the events five years after they have occurred. The perspectives created for the two "narrators" are then comparable in the distancing they provide, but whereas Tom looks at the past from the point of view of an adult who has survived it, the poet of Crane's work looks at it through the eyes of the child who is still undergoing the events.

[28]Paul, *Hart's Bridge,* p. 125.

[29]In his essay "On A Streetcar Named Success" (1947), reprinted in *Where I Lived,* eds. Day and Woods, p. 22.

[30]Paul, *Hart's Bridge,* p. 129.

[31]As the speaker in the poem is "conscripted" to the "shadows' glow" of the decanters (*Poems,* p. 92).

[32]Lewis, *Hart Crane,* p. 193.

The Glass Menagerie:
From Story to Play

Lester A. Beaurline

"Not even daring to stretch her small hands out!—nobody, not even the rain, has such small hands." Tennessee Williams scrawled these words from e. e. cummings at the top of the last page of *The Glass Menagerie* sometime after finishing the one-act play that was to grow into his first successful work. The quotation suggests the gentle, elegiac tone that he tried to attain, and since the last half of the passage survived as the play's epigraph, it apparently expressed Williams' later feelings too. The fragile pathos of Laura Wingfield's life was Williams' original inspiration in his short story, "Portrait of a Girl in Glass," and theater audiences continue to respond to the basic human appeal of the play.

In "Portrait" the narrator feels compassion for Laura, who "made no positive motion toward the world but stood at the edge of the water, so to speak, with feet that anticipated too much cold to move." In this early story we can already recognize Williams' other trademarks: the theme of Tom's flight from "a dead but beautiful past into a live but ugly and meaningless present" (William Sharp, *TDR*, VI, March, 1962, 161), the images of leaves torn from their branches, the hundreds of little transparent pieces of glass, the tired old music of the dead past, and the emotional undercurrent of sexual passion roaring through the entire story. These themes, I suppose, show Williams' kinship with D. H. Lawrence; and Tom, no doubt, suggests the figure of Paul Morrell or Aaron Sisson. But the later revisions show Williams' real talents as a playwright, none of which he inherits from Lawrence: his breadth of sympathy, his sense of humor, his brilliant dialogue, and his talent for building highly charged dramatic scenes.

"*The Glass Menagerie*: From Stage to Play" by Lester A. Beaurline. From *Modern Drama*, 8 (1965), 142–49. Copyright © 1965 *Modern Drama*. Reprinted by permission of the author and the publisher.

Evidence survives for at least four stages in the composition of *The Glass Menagerie:* (1) The sixteen page story entitled "Portrait of a Girl in Glass" (written before 1943 and published in *One Arm and Other Stories,* 1948), where attention is on Laura, the narrator's sister.

(2) A sixty page one-act play in five scenes, of which twenty-one pages survive in the C. Waller Barrett Library at the University of Virginia. It is clear from the existing fragments (embedded in the manuscript of the longer version described below) that Williams had the main lines of his play firmly in hand at this stage. Here the clash between Tom and Amanda, the painful relationship between Amanda and Laura, and the contrast between Jim and Tom have become as important as Laura herself. This script was probably written before Williams went to California to work on a movie script in 1943 and before he worked up a synopsis for a film named *The Gentleman Caller* (Nancy Tischler, *Tennessee Williams,* p. 92).

(3) A 105-page play manuscript, now in the C. Waller Barrett Library at the University of Virginia. This complex document contains ten kinds of paper, is written on at least six different typewriters and has four different kinds of handwritten pencil or ink revisions. It may represent about eight to ten layers of revision, but for the sake of clarity, I will refer to only the final stage of the third version: the manuscript as it stood when Williams sent it off to his agent in the fall of 1943. He called this the "reading version," and it is very close to the Random House edition, published in 1945 and reprinted by New Directions in 1949. However, this printed edition (which unfortunately has gotten into the college anthologies) contains several errors and a few alterations. The long version of the manuscript is in seven scenes and is a development and expansion of episodes in the one-act version. At this stage the major emphasis in the play is on memory, Tom's memory. It is a play about growing up as Tom must recognize the fatal choice between Laura's glass animals and Jim's gross materialism.

(4) The acting version, published by the Dramatists Play Service in 1948 (and revised again sometime in the mid-fifties). This purports to be "a faithful indication of the way the play was produced in New York and on the road" by the original company. Many changes have been made in the stage directions and details of the dialogue. Thirteen new speeches were added to scene four, and over 1100 verbal changes appear in the dialogue alone. I think that Williams is now finished with the play and that the fourth version

represents his final intentions. Therefore a responsible editor of an anthology should *not* reprint the old "reading version," and a critic ignores the acting version at his peril.

Changes in Tom's last speech epitomize all the revision in the play, so it is worth examining a long passage that closes the "Girl in Glass."

> Not very long after that I lost my job at the warehouse. I was fired for writing a poem on the lid of a shoe-box. I left Saint Louis and took to moving around. The cities swept about me like dead leaves, leaves that were brightly colored but torn away from the branches. My nature changed. I grew to be firm and sufficient.
>
> In five years' time I had nearly forgotten home. I had to forget it, I couldn't carry it with me. But once in a while, usually in a strange town before I have found companions, the shell of deliberate hardness is broken through. A door comes softly and irresistibly open. I hear the tired old music my unknown father left in the place he abandoned as faithlessly as I. I see the faint and sorrowful radiance of the glass, hundreds of little transparent pieces of it in very delicate colors. I hold my breath, for if my sister's face appears among them—the night is hers! (pp. 111–112, by permission of New Directions Books)

In the second draft (the one-act version), Williams heightened Tom's emotional tension between his necessary cruelty and his affection for the ones he is hurting. His cruel side comes out when he says, "Then I escaped. Without a word of goodbye, I descended the steps of the fire-escape for the last time." The incestuous implications of the speech become more explicit: "In five years time I have nearly forgotten home. But there are nights when memory is stronger. I cannot hold my shoulder to the door, the door comes softly but irresistibly open. . . . I hold my breath. I reach for a cigarette. I buy a drink, I speak to the nearest stranger, For if that vision goes on growing clearer, the mist will divide upon my sister's face, watching gently and daring to ask for nothing. Then it's too much: my manhood is undone and the night is hers. . . ." [MS p. 103 (60); the number in parenthesis refers to the original pagination of the one-act play; the other number refers to the revised pagination of the "reading version."]

In the third version, the speech is more integrated with the scene. Amanda had just shouted at him, "Go then! Then go to the moon!—you selfish dreamer." So Tom begins his epilogue with "I didn't go to the moon. I went much further—for time is the longest distance between two places." (We should recall that Amanda had asked Laura to wish on the moon before the gentleman caller came.) Another unifying detail was added at the end. Laura, in pantomime, blows out the candles, which like the moon have come to suggest her hopes, the romantic half-light, similar to the glow that came across the alley from the Paradise Ballroom. She had already blown out her candles in the second version, but in the third, Tom says, "anything that can blow your candles out! (LAURA BENDS OVER THE CANDLES) Blow out your candles, Laura!—for nowadays the world is lit by lightning! Blow out your candles, Laura,—and so goodbye. . . . (SHE BLOWS THE CANDLES OUT. THE SCENE DISSOLVES.)" (MS pp. 104–105) So the dialogue and action reinforce each other.

Also in the third version Tom gives a more concrete impression of the memory of his sister. He suggests a little dramatic scene where he is no longer in a bedroom with his shoulder to the door. Perhaps the lines from e. e. cummings stimulated an impression of out-of-doors rather than a bedroom. Tom says, "Perhaps I am walking along a street at night, in some strange city, before I have found companions. I pass the lighted window of a shop where perfume is sold. The window is filled with pieces of colored glass, tiny transparent bottles in delicate colors, like bits of a shattered rainbow.

Then all at once my sister touches my shoulder. I turn around and look into her eyes. . . .

Oh, Laura, Laura, I tried to leave you behind me, but I am more faithful than I intended to be!"

The fourth or acting version emphasizes Tom's maturity and cruelty even more; now Tom leaves out all mention of his being fired from his job at the warehouse. The impression is that he voluntarily left home—to join the merchant marine. His costume, on stage, has become a pea jacket and a watch-cap, again combining the dialogue and the spectacle.

Joining the merchant marine represents his escape into freedom, his escape from a box; and the second and third versions for the whole play show the regular growth of this theme. To draw the light away from the relations of Tom and Laura and towards an inevitable clash between Tom and Amanda, Williams wrote a long argument into the early scenes. Amanda accuses Tom of being selfish, not caring for his poor sister, and Tom replies vehemently. The first half of this passage is, as many other speeches in the manuscript, in loose blank verse, which the printed texts obscure.

> Listen! You think I'm *crazy* about the *warehouse?*
> You think I'm in love with the Continental Shoemakers?
> You think I want to spend fifty-five *years* down there in that—*celotex interior*! with—*flourescent*—*tubes*?!
> Look! I'd rather somebody picked up a crow-bar and battered out my brains—than go back mornings! I *GO*! Everytime you come in yelling that God damn *'Rise and Shine! Rise and Shine!'* I say to myself, 'How *lucky dead* people are!' (MS p. 28, by permission of Random House and the University of Virginia Library)

As J. L. Styan (*Elements of Drama,* p. 12) observed, good dramatic speech has had a "specific pressure put on it"; it is economical because it functions in several ways at the same time. This speech not only furthers the action, but it characterizes Tom, the frustrated poet, who sees his work and his home as a box where he endures a living death, surrounded by phoniness and clichés. But the audience is also aware of Amanda's reaction, because we have just seen how she suffers, in her comitragic telephone conversations, while she tries to sell magazines in order to put her daughter through business college. Meantime Laura spends her days walking in the park or polishing her glass. Neither does Williams let us forget Laura during the big argument. In the third version, a spotlight shines upon her tense body; in the fourth version, she stands in the living room, at the door of the dining room, overhearing the whole exchange. Thus she is between the audience and the action in the dining room.

Then before Tom storms out of the apartment, he flings his coat across the room, *"It strikes against the shelf of Laura's glass collection, there is a tinkle of shattering glass. Laura cries out as if wounded."* This stage business is an obvious parallel with the accident that occurs in the next act at the end of Laura and Jim's dance, when the little glass unicorn is broken, just before Jim reveals that he is engaged to marry. He can never call on Laura again.

Scene four, with the only extensive addition that was written for the acting version (but printed in the Random House edition and absent from the Barrett MS) also emphasizes the choice that Tom has between death and escape. Tom has come home from the movies, where he gets his adventure, and he describes the magician in the stage show. "But the wonderfullest trick of all was the coffin trick. We nailed him into a coffin and he got out of the coffin without removing one nail. There is a trick that would come in handy for me—get out of this 2 by 4 situation. . . . You know it don't take much intelligence to get yourself into a nailed-up coffin, Laura. But who in hell ever got himself out of one without removing one nail? *(As an answer, the father's grinning photograph lights up.)* "

There are a hundred ways that the body of the play depicts Tom's awareness of the essential hopelessness of the Wingfield family and the essential deadness of their beautiful memories. I will not explain how each detail came into the script; two more examples will have to suffice. One of the greatest moments in modern theater occurs when Amanda comes on stage to greet Laura's gentleman caller. Nobody says a word for a few seconds; everyone's eyes are fixed on Amanda's dress—the old ball dress that she wore when she led the cotillion years ago. Before age had yellowed this dress she had twice won the cakewalk, and she had worn it to the Governor's ball in Jackson. The dress, at this moment, suggests the utter futility of Amanda's efforts to find a husband for her daughter. She defeats her own purposes; she cannot resist pretending that the gentleman caller has come to call on her, just as seventeen of them came one afternoon on Blue Mountain. Tom is shocked and embarrassed. The grotesque sight leaves Jim speechless, and he is a young man proud of his high-school training in public speaking. Meanwhile Laura lies in her bedroom, sick with fear.

Mr. Williams did not achieve such a theatrical triumph by writing with his guts or by pouring out his uncontrolled libido. In the short story, he tried to make Laura pathetic by dressing her in one of her mother's old gowns, and Tom is momentarily surprised by her appearance when she opens the door. In the one-act version, Amanda's memories of Blue Mountain are written into the script, and Laura is furnished with a new dress, but now she is lame. By the third version (possibly in the second, too, but I cannot be sure because the relevant pages of the second version do not survive), Amanda wears the old dress and becomes a coquette. In the fourth version, Williams softens the effect slightly and adds a little more to the irony by a brief exchange between Tom and his mother. At the peak of Tom's embarrassment, after the pregnant pause, he says:

Mother, you look so pretty.
Amanda: You know, that's the first compliment you ever

paid me. I wish you'd look pleasant when you're
about to say something pleasant, so I could expect it.

Then Amanda swings into her girlish chatter. These last additions
seem to assure the audience that Tom is genuinely shocked but that
he is trying to cover up his feelings. At the same time the audience
has to have evidence that Amanda is not completely out of her
mind. She can still recognize a hollow compliment, and she can
return the jibe.

By typical use of his dramatic talents, Williams makes the
audience conscious of several characters' feelings at the same time,
like a juggler keeping four balls in the air. Each revision puts
another ball in the air or increases the specific pressure. We are
never allowed to forget the tension between Tom and his mother,
and the scene strongly suggests that Laura's anxiety and withdrawal
may have been caused by her aggressive mother. The final image of
Amanda in the Epilogue is that of a comforter and protector of
Laura. She is dignified and tragic. But she is most vividly depicted in
the middle of the play as a vigorous, silly, and pathetic old woman.
Fearing that her daughter might become an old maid, she arranges
the visit of a gentleman caller. Yet, she cannot resist the temptation
to smother her daughter and relive her Blue Mountain days; she
vicariously seduces the man herself. She has to keep bringing the
dead but beautiful past into the present; Tom must go into the ugly
but live future. He must break out of the coffin and leave his sister
behind in darkness.

The transmutations of Jim O'Connor illustrate Mr. Williams'
talent for depicting minor characters. At the start, Jim had a warm
masculine nature; he was a potential lover and a Lawrencian hero.
"Jim was a big red-haired Irishman who had the scrubbed and
polished look of well-kept chinaware. His big square hands seemed
to have a direct and very innocent hunger for touching friends. He
was always clapping them on your arms or shoulders and they
burned through the cloth of your shirt like plates taken out of an
oven."

In the one-act version, Jim becomes slightly hollow when he tries
to persuade Tom to study public speaking. Then, in the reading
version, Jim assimilates some of the play's nostalgic tone when he
becomes an ex-high-school hero. The distracting homosexual
suggestions disappear, and now Tom was "valuable to him as
someone who could remember his former glory, who had seen him

win basketball games and the silver cup in debating." On the edge of failure, Jim seems to put on his hearty good nature. He is more often named the "gentleman caller" than Jim O'Connor, a detail that helps to transform him into an idea in the head of Amanda, just as Laura becomes an image of "Blue-roses" in his mind. Also in the reading version Jim first talks enthusiastically about the world of the present and future—the world that Amanda and Laura cannot enter. When he should be romancing with Laura, he orates on the Wrigley Building, the Century of Progress, and the future of television. "I wish to be ready to go up right along with it. Therefore I'm planning to get in on the ground floor. In fact I've already made the right connections and all that remains is for the industry itself to get under way! Full steam—*(His eyes are starry.) Knowledge*—Zzzzzp! *Money*—Zzzzzp!—*Power!* That's the cycle democracy is built on!" He clumsily breaks Laura's unicorn, and he awkwardly kisses her.

Jim finally impresses us as a dehumanized figure, an unromantic voice of power and cliché; his sex appeal has been carefully removed, and his insensitive words and power of positive thinking take its place. Consequently, with every change he suits Laura less and less, and he embodies Tom's "celotex interior" more and more. In the finished play, Amanda's mental projection of the old-fashioned gentleman caller reveals him to be Tom's brute reality.

Other important changes are found in the stage directions, especially the visual images and printed legends that Williams experimented with and rejected—wisely, I think. One legend, "A Souvenir," survives in the fragments of the one-act play (at the beginning of what was eventually scene viii), and the earliest forms of the reading version show an attempted use of a blackboard on which Tom wrote in chalk such things as *"Blue Roses"* (scene ii), *"Campaign"* (scene iii), and *"Où sont les Neiges d'antan"* (scene i). The completed reading version projected these legends by means of the much discussed "screen device," possibly conceived in the film synopsis that preceded the reading version. Williams said, "The legend or image upon the screen will strengthen the effect of what is merely allusion [*sic*] in the writing and allow the primary point to be made more simply and lightly than if the entire responsibility were on the spoken lines" (New Directions edition, 1949, p. x). The real weakness of the device lies in the author's anxiousness and small confidence in his audience. "In an episodic play, such as this, the basic structure or narrative line may be obscured from the audience; the effect may seem fragmentary rather than architectural. This may not be the fault of the play so much as a lack of attention in the audience" (p. x). And I suspect that if the screen device has ever been tried, it distracted the audience from the actors, just as the lighting can distract unless it is used sparingly. Father's lighted picture seems to work once or twice, but I doubt if similar mechanical marvels add to the effect. At any rate, Williams says he does not regret the omission of the screen device in the first New York production, because he saw that Laurette Taylor's powerful performance "made it suitable to have the utmost simplicity in physical production" (p. x). Jo Mielziner's two scrims no doubt also helped persuade him. An air of unreality is one thing but pretentious pointing out of meaning is another.

Williams' most successful revisions of stage directions unobtrusively change the story's matter-of-fact tone into memory. The narrator of the story becomes the presenter of the play, and significant stage properties appear in the big scene: the blasted candelabra from the altar of the Church of the Heavenly Rest, the ice cream, fruit punch, and macaroons. In the reading version the ice cream was replaced with dandelion wine (for a mock communion?), and Amanda "baptizes" herself with lemonade—all of which contributes to the vaguely religious impression of the scene. No one explicitly defines the meaning of these symbols, but they quietly suggest that the events represent Laura's pitiful initiation rites; this is as close as she will ever come to the altar of love, because Jim is no Savior. She must blow her candles out, for the empty ceremony is over.

The Texas Drafts
of *The Glass Menagerie*

R. B. Parker

Lester Beaurline's lucid appraisal of the Williams manuscripts in the Barrett Library of the University of Virginia pioneered the analysis of *Menagerie*'s development[1]; but since his article appeared, a great deal of extra material has been deposited at the Humanities Research Centre of the University of Texas which shows that the genesis of the play was even more complex than he supposed. This new material is largely undated, however, and thus far has only been sorted out by text; so until an accurate time sequence can be worked out among the many drafts (and the Texas material collated with the archive in Virginia), nothing like a definitive analysis will be possible. Nevertheless, certain details are already clear that can affect interpretation of the finished play.

For example, it is usually assumed that *Menagerie* developed directly from the screenplay called *The Gentleman Caller,* but a glance at the screenplay itself shows that this can only have been true in part. Texas has two copies of Williams' general *Description* of the screenplay dated May 13, 1943 (plus 6 extra pages of draft, dated June 28, 1943), and a more elaborate but undated *Provisional Story Treatment* that recently turned up there during sorting of the David Selznick papers. The *Description* has no narrator but opens with a lengthy account of Amanda's life at Blue Mountain, her gentlemen callers, Wingfield's wooing, and his misadventure with an illicit still, which forced the family to leave town. The "play" proper then begins on Christmas Eve with Laura, who is "morbidly shy" but not in this version lame, decorating a tree while her brother "Larry"

"The Texas Drafts of *The Glass Menagerie,*" by R. B. Parker, excerpted from "The Composition of *The Glass Menagerie:* An Argument for Complexity," *Modern Drama* (September, 1982). Copyright © 1982 *Modern Drama.* Reprinted by permission of the author and the publisher. Quotations from the Texas archive are by permission of Tennessee Williams and the Humanities Research Centre, The University of Texas at Austin.

reads poetry aloud; they attempt to attract passing carollers with a candle at the window; and Amanda gives them unsuitable Christmas presents, a six-month business course for Laura and books on salesmanship and "executive personality" for Larry. Laura fails at business college largely because she is bullied by a "hawklike spinster" instructor. Larry's restlessness is explained by the fact that "The Wingfields . . . were pioneers, Indian fighters, trail blazers in the American wilderness," and there is "an amusing incidental scene" in which one of his wanderlust poems wins a $10.00 prize from the Ladies' Wednesday Club. Laura likes the gentleman caller, Jim, because his freckles remind her of the hero of her favorite Gene Stratton Porter novel (as in "Portrait"), not because she knew him in high school; the lights do not go off, there is no Paradise Dance Hall, little is made of the glass collection, and there is no unicorn to be broken. As in *Stairs to the Roof,* Larry loses his job for smoking on the roof, not for writing poems on cartons; and on the morning after his departure, Laura tries to comfort her mother by volunteering to phone for magazine subscriptions, but does so too early—at 6:30 a.m.—which makes them both laugh and restores Amanda's morale.

The *Provisional Story Treatment* is even further from *Menagerie.* It is divided into three parts linked by an unidentified narrator. Part I dramatizes events at Blue Mountain, with scenes of gentlemen callers visiting Amanda, her first meeting with Wingfield, his proposal at a picnic and fight with another of her admirers, her snubbing of his next visit but sudden decision to elope with him. The narrator then bridges to a hotel in Memphis where Amanda watches boats go down the river and tells Wingfield of her first pregnancy. Wingfield enlists for World War I and Amanda, pregnant with his second child, returns to Blue Mountain. Wingfield comes home a shell-shocked hero but begins bootlegging, and an elaborate sequence follows in which his still blows up, killing a Negro, and bloodhounds track him to his father-in-law's church. The dogs attack Laura on the church steps, and Wingfield, rescuing her, is arrested and taken to prison. Part II tells of the family's life in St. Louis, with the embittered father working in a shirt factory. Laura has been so traumatized by the bloodhounds that she cannot talk until her father delights her into speech by bringing home a victrola on which he plays *Dardanella.* Amanda objects to the expense of this, and Wingfield leaves for good. The narrator then tells of the children growing up over shots of Tom (in this version) reading magazines instead of selling them and brooding despairingly in a warehouse, Amanda selling subscriptions over the phone, and Laura having nightmares about dogs, failing to recite at school, playing *Dardanella,* polishing her glass collection, and endlessly rereading *Freckles.* Part III covers the same sequence as the *Description,* beginning with the Christmas Eve scene. Once more Laura is bullied by her typing instructor, but now the machine clatter is described as sounding like "hounds baying." There is no poetry prize scene, but again Laura likes Jim solely because of his freckles and again there is no unicorn. Tom's speech on leaving home is now made to echo his father's earlier recriminations; and after the scene in which Laura makes her comically early phone call, three alternative endings are suggested: Either Amanda and Laura will return to Blue Mountain where Laura insists her mother is "just as beautiful as she was—in the beginning"; or Laura will be shown welcoming hosts of gentlemen callers at Blue Mountain, like her mother earlier; or one or other of the Tom Wingfields will return: "At any rate—Amanda has finally found security and rest. What she searched for in the faces of Gentlemen Callers." This *Story Treatment* is carelessly typed, and since it is in a Liebling-Wood folder and Part III announces that it "covers the part of the story contained in the stage play 'The Gentleman Caller' ('The Glass Menagerie')," possibly it was cobbled up either before or just after the New York opening of *Menagerie* when Selznick was alerted to take an interest in the play. Its differences from *Menagerie* suggest, though, that it drew on earlier material.

The discrepancies relate back, in fact, to the stage play of *The Gentleman Caller,* which survives in many partial versions but no complete one. The Texas archive contains multiple overlapping drafts, including a 22-page fragment with the title *The Gentleman Caller, or Portrait of a girl in glass (A lyric play),* 29 disorderly pages called *The Gentleman Caller (original and only copy of a rather tiresome play)* and subtitled *(the ruins of a play),* another 20-page fragment entitled *The Gentleman Caller (A Gentle Comedy),* and a composite typescript of 156 pages, plus 40 pages of pencil draft in a notebook and some 254 further draft pages in typescript. Names and details change bewilderingly throughout these drafts: Laura is sometimes called Rose or Rosemary (and once Miriam) and varies between 18, 20, and 23 in age; Tom is often called Larry; Jim has several Irish

surnames and hails variously from Oregon, Nebraska, or Wyoming;
and the St. Louis apartment is located on Maple Street, Enright, or,
most often, Côte Brilliante Avenue.

The confusion reflects the trouble Williams had controlling his
material. "It's the hardest thing I have ever tried to say!" Tom
assures the audience in the "ruins of a play,"

> I've written this over ten times and torn it up, I've sweated over it,
> raged over it, wept over it! I think I have it and then it gets all misty
> and fades away. . . . I must confine myself to a smaller ambition,
> not all but a little of it.[2]

Similarly, in the notebook pencil draft Tom says:

> The original play filled several hundred pages. The top heavy
> structure collapsed. And I lay under the ruins like a caterpillar. After
> a while I picked myself up again. I looked about me. Here and there I
> picked up a sound particle, a piece that survived. I put these
> fragments together. Out of the ruins of a monument salvaged this
> tablet, these remnants of a play, *The Gentleman Caller.*

This shortened version of *The Gentleman Caller* corresponded
closely, but again not exactly, to the *Description* of the film script,[3]
and the sequence is complicated further by his trying-out sections
of the material also as one-acts. *The Pretty Trap (A Comedy in One Act),*
for instance, has the title-page note "This play is derived from a
longer work in progress, *The Gentleman Caller.* It corresponds to the
last act of that play, roughly, but has a lighter treatment and a
different end." Jim's visit here takes place on Sadie Hawkins day
(when girls can propose to men); Laura is shy but not lame; the
lights, however, do go out, much more is made of the glass animals
than in the film script, and the unicorn appears but is not broken.
After Jim's kiss he mentions no fiancée but asks if he can take Laura
for a walk; and when they have left, Amanda ends the play exulting
to Tom, "Girls are a pretty trap! That's what they've always been,
and always will *be,* even when *dreams* plus *action*—take over the
world: Now—now, dreamy type—Let's finish the dishes!" A
similar ending occurs in the full-length *The Gentleman Caller (A Gentle
Comedy),* with the addition that Amanda tells Tom to take out the
suitcase he has hidden under his bed and leave now with her
blessing, "Then come home and I'll be waiting for you—no matter
how long!"

Other one-acts that seem to have preceded either version of *The*

Gentleman Caller are "Carollers, our Candle" (dated April 1943), which covers the Christmas Eve sequence,[4] and the fragmentary "A Daughter of the Revolution (A Comedy)," dated March 1943 and inscribed to "Miss Lilian and Miss Dorothy Gish for either of whom the part of Amanda Wingfield was hopefully intended by the author," which presents Amanda's comic telephone subscriptions. Another early one-act, "If You Breathe, It Breaks! or Portrait of a Girl in Glass" takes place at Blue Mountain, where Mrs. Wingfield is represented as the widow of an Episcopal clergyman, supporting her family by running a boarding house; Rosemary, her shy, plain daughter, is teased by malicious borders and treated badly by a younger brother Ronald, but is taken off to the White Star Pharmacy for a soda by a middle-aged widower, Mr. Wallard, to whom she gives her prized glass unicorn. Another, more farcical Blue Mountain one-act, "With Grace and Dignity or The Memorial Service," included among *The Gentleman Caller* drafts, depicts Rosemary's inability to carry a white taper during Mrs. Wingfield's celebration of her election as Regent of the local chapter of the D.A.R. and the substitution for her of the Negro cook with a candle stub from the kitchen.

What one needs to understand from this welter of alternatives is the difficulty Williams had in coming to terms with his material and the complexity of his responses to it, because clearly there was no steady progression in one direction—details come and go bewilderingly—and though in *Menagerie* he found a form that brilliantly controls the material, some of the rejected alternatives are still faintly there, like an imaginative penumbra.

For instance, in drafts of the longer version of the stage *Gentleman Caller,* one can trace his efforts to "place" the story. One recurring experiment is to try to set it within a "pioneer" framework, recounting the Williams family history in Sandburg-like verse at the beginning (against a large map of America) and returning to it at the end to explain the necessity of Tom's choice and to reassure the audience of the women's ability to survive "because we're daughters of the Revolution." The same element comes up more obliquely in a version where Williams introduces a young vagrant, Tom Lee, whom Amanda invites to breakfast when she finds him stealing milk bottles, then dismisses to the fire escape again for "bolshevik" opinions, only to find that Tom prefers to join him there; and in another draft it is one of Williams' "fugitive kind," a street-musician called Tony, who calls Amanda disrespectfully "Mother

Wing" and is dismissed by her as an "artistic bum", who persuades Tom to join the merchant marine and leave the stolid Jim to take his room and place in the family.[5] A related experiment has the play remembered by Tom himself sleeping in a doss house and deciding to return home when he hears carollers outside. Shades of this left-wing comment and romantic bohemianism remain in the Tom of *Menagerie,* but in a more qualified, ironic tone that is linked to another of Williams' experiments in *The Gentleman Caller*—the theatricalism of a framework in which Tom criticizes the lighting man and at several points argues directly with the audience in justification of the play. The combative, slightly aggressive relation to the audience in these last experiments is worth remembering.

A different kind of framework tries to set the children within a context of their parents, showing Amanda's relationship with Wingfield at the beginning and, in at least two versions, having the husband return to resolve the situation at the end; and this reflects a different kind of light that the drafts can shed on *Glass Menagerie.* Critics react so sympathetically to the Wingfields that they are apt to miss shades of characterization, but familiarity with the earlier attempts alerts us to Williams' own ambivalences, particularly his unexpected siding with his father. Amanda can be very sympathetic, as Williams surely meant her to be, but she is also grotesquely comic, and the drafts often emphasize this—by the story of the exploding still, for instance, which in some versions Tom uses to deflate her reminiscences of Blue Mountain, or the description of her waiting up for him in a dingy flannel wrapper, "smelling of Vicks' Vap-o-rub—a portrait of Motherhood that would make Whistler turn in his grave." There is also a certain flexibility in the presentation of Laura. Besides varying her age and only occasionally making her lame, Williams presents her with very different degrees of neuresthenia, ranging from completely fey fantasies that she and Tom will escape to Freckles' "Limberlost" in a blue coupé and live together in an old, abandoned house, to a degree of moral strength that enables her to assure Tom that she will not be harmed by the disappointment of Jim or by Tom's departure and to take over when her mother finally breaks down. And in the curious version with the street-musician Tony, she is transformed to a highly strung member of the local Little Theatre who wants to be "Duse! Bernhardt! Duncan! Pavlova! Garbo! Joan of Arc!" with a sharp, sarcastic tongue that is more than a match for her mother's, while it is Tom who is the withdrawn and quiet one.

This interesting transfer of identities was anticipated in the one-act "The Long Goodbye" in which it is the promiscuous sister who is forced from home and the poetic brother who finds it difficult to leave, and it also prefigures characterization in the revised version of *The Two Character Play* more recently.

Most important of all, however, is the draft versions' evidence that Williams was uncertain how to end the story and was constantly tempted to use optimistic conclusions, ranging from loud assertions of American independence, through happy returns of Wingfield Senior, Tom, or Jim, to attempts to show the women prospering in some way on their own. With hindsight, we can see that Williams was right to discard these experiments, but it is important to bear them in mind when, for instance, we consider the sentimental conclusion of the 1950 film, in which Laura, cured by her encounter with Jim, has her pick of gentleman callers "And the one she chose was named Richard."[6] It is usual to blame this travesty onto Hollywood, noting that the script is credited to Williams and a rewrite man named Peter Berneis. But we have seen Williams experimenting with such conclusions in his drafts,[7] and Texas has a film script of *The Glass Menagerie* by Williams alone in which Laura, cutting business school, makes friends with a little girl sketching in the Botanical Gardens and eventually falls happily in love with the child's sympathetic art teacher. To do Williams justice, he has scrawled across the cover of this script, "A Horrible Thing! Certified by Tennessee Williams."

A similar caution must be exercised with changes introduced into the original production and subsequently enshrined in the Dramatists Playservice acting edition. The director, Eddie Dowling (who also played Tom), influenced by George Jean Nathan, thought the play was not funny enough and introduced Tom's drunken return in scene 4. According to Williams, Dowling wanted Tom to sing "My Melancholy Baby" and swig from a red, white, and blue flask,[8] but though Williams agreed to include the scene, he wrote it in his own way, weaving it into the pattern of the play by its motifs of rainbow scarf, magician, coffin, and escape. Actually the play is full of humor, but it is of Williams' own oblique and mordant kind. He credits Laurette Taylor with a special gift for this sort of wild, black comedy and it was because she could balance it so carefully against Amanda's sympathetic qualities that he allowed her many small revisions of lines that, without the counterbalance she provided, can combine to make Amanda overly sympathetic.[9] Much the same reason may also have influenced him in permitting the projection of titles to be cut. To my knowledge, the play has only once been produced as originally intended, and that quite recently and in German;[10] nonetheless Williams insisted that the Random House–New Directions reading edition largely return to his original script. He has been criticized for doing this,[11] but, when we remember his laborious experiments through draft after draft of *The Gentleman Caller*, searching for the proper framework, it seems probable that he was as right to do so as he was later in printing the original end to *Cat on a Hot Tin Roof* that Elia Kazan had sentimentalized in production. To insist, as most critics still do,[12] that the projection device is jejune or pretentious is to do Williams and his play an injustice.

Notes

[1] Lester A. Beaurline, *"The Glass Menagerie:* From Story to Play," *Modern Drama,* 8 (September 1965), 142–149.

[2] My ellipsis; the speech is a very long one.

[3] Cf. Williams's "scenic out-line of the playscript" in an undated letter to Audrey Wood, reproduced in Richard F. Leavitt, *The World of Tennessee Williams* (New York: Putnams, 1978), pp. 52–3.

[4] This may be the earliest element in *The Gentleman Caller*. The Texas archive has a note scribbled on two loose sheets in what looks like a very early, juvenile hand, recording a brother's musing about what his sister can be thinking as she decorates a Christmas tree.

[5] Jim is characterized in much the same way in *Stairs to the Roof.*

[6] *Screen Hits Annual,* no. 5 (1950), p. 50.

[7] As he also did with happy endings for *Streetcar;* cf. Vivienne Dickson, *"A Streetcar Named Desire:* Its Development through the Manuscripts," in *Tennessee Williams: A Tribute,* ed. Jac Tharpe (Jackson: University Press of Mississippi, 1977) p. 157.

[8] *Memoirs,* p. 82; Mrs. Williams remembers the song as the bawdiest verse of *The St. Louis Blues:* op. cit., p. 145.

[9] See James L. Rowland, "Tennessee's Two Amandas," *Research Studies* (Washington State University), 35 (1971), 331–40, though Professor Rowland prefers the revised, sympathetic version.

[10] Cf. Christian Jauslin, *Tennessee Williams—Dramatiker Welttheaters,* Vol. 59 (München: Friedrich Verlag, 1976), pp. 123–5, 129. I am indebted to Professor Debusscher for this reference.

[11] See, for instance, Lester Beaurline, "The Director, the Script, and Author's Revisions: A Critical Problem," *Papers in Dramatic Theory and Criticism,* ed. David M. Knauf (University of Iowa Press, 1969), p. 89.

[12] e.g. Beaurline, "The Director . . ."; S. Alan Chesler, "Tennessee Williams: Reassessment and Assessment," in Tharpe, p. 853; Mary Ann Corrigan, "Beyond

Verisimilitude: Echoes of Expressionism in Williams' Plays," *Ibid.,* 392. A notable early argument against this attitude can be found in George Brandt, "Cinematic Structure in the work of Tennessee Williams," in *American Theatre,* ed. J. R. Brown and B. Harris (London: Edward Arnold, 1967), pp. 184–5.

Tennessee's Two Amandas

James L. Rowland

Tennessee Williams' first successful play, *The Glass Menagerie,* has become one of the most popular dramas of the first half of this century and is produced more frequently than any other play in high schools, colleges, and community theatre groups. It has also been revived year after year on Broadway, and it had special revivals in honor of its tenth and twentieth anniversaries. It has been widely anthologized and has been included in many high school and college literature courses.

Despite this popularity, the astonishing fact remains that there are really two plays, not one, and that those who read the play are reading not merely a different *Glass Menagerie,* but, I believe, a distinctly inferior one. The problem is significant not only for this play, but for the general question arising in the reading of all dramatic literature: Which version is correct, which version represents the author's final intention?

The problem is nearly as complicated as any study of a Shakespearean folio, and confusion and error are abundant in the record. The first question is: What version are we talking about? For simplicity's sake, let us designate two—the so-called "reading version," found in most anthologies and copyrighted in 1945, and the so-called "acting version," seldom reprinted except through the Dramatists Play Service and copyrighted in 1948.

A background of the development of the play has been outlined by Lester A. Beaurline,[1] who traces its growth from a short story and loses it somewhere in the fog of "revised again sometime in the mid-fifties."[2] In short, there was an unpublished version copyrighted (as an unpublished play) in 1945; in that same year a copyrighted, published version appeared: the "reading version" found in most anthologies. This version is distinguished immediately by the elaborate introduction of the characters, and by the intricate "magic lantern" stage business, which the author's introduction tells the reader was never used. Williams explains further that the only important difference between the reading and the acting versions of the play is the omission of the screen device, a statement which I find impossible to accept. In 1948 the "acting version," produced in 1945, was copyrighted and published. I am concerned here with the confusion caused by the existence of two published versions of the play, and the significant reasons for believing that only one of them, the "acting version," should be regarded as representing the real *Glass Menagerie*.

This confusion has infected criticism. Signi Lenea Falk refers to the *Glass Menagerie* as "a memory play, a series of seven sharply remembered scenes," and a conversation is quoted from the "reading version" of the play. However, Falk's note for this discussion actually refers to the "acting version"![3] Beaurline's confusion has already been noted. At least one publisher of a college anthology of drama has printed the 1948 copyrighted and published version of the play with the 1945 copyright date of the "reading version."[4] This is not only a bibliographical mistake but could turn out to be an involved financial error for the publisher, since the production restrictions that apply to all acting versions are not indicated in the anthology.

More important, however, is the question of which play should we read as the author's final intention. The "acting version" is my choice, not because it is a later version, but because the characters are more fully developed, and more understandable. Beaurline states that there are more than "1100 verbal changes." The count is probably accurate; yet it is the significance of the changes I wish to discuss. Beaurline presents a few examples of changes that were made in Tom. In this study I shall use Amanda in order to show the transition the play makes from its "reading" to its "acting version," for it is my belief that she is the character in the drama to whom the other participants react. Changes made in Amanda often necessitate changes in the other characters.

The "reading version" used here is found in the college anthology *Representative Modern Plays: American,* Robert Warnock, editor, Scott, Foresman and Co., 1952, pp. 587–653. The "acting version" is found in the college anthology *Nine Modern American Plays,* Barrett H. Clark, editor, Appleton-Century-Crofts, Inc., 1951, pp. 341–379.

The first revision appears on the first page. In the "reading version" Amanda, under the heading characters, is described as,

Amanda Wingfield (the mother)
A little woman of great but confused vitality clinging frantically to another time and place. Her characterization must be carefully created, not copied from type. She is not paranoiac, but her life is paranoia. There is much to admire in Amanda, and as much to love and pity as there is to laugh at. Certainly she has endurance and a kind of heroism, and though her foolishness makes her unwittingly cruel at times, there is tenderness in her slight person. (p. 587)

In the "acting version" all that is listed under characters is "The Mother" (p. 341). The above description, at first viewing, seems like a necessary explanation. As one compares these two versions, however, it becomes evident that Williams, through revision and expansion of Amanda's lines in the "acting version," took care of the extensive introduction within the play. The production notes for the "reading version" are also long and detailed. By the time the "acting version" was published, most of these had been eliminated. Nearly all of Williams' suggested production techniques and devices were cut out by directors.

The changes continue at the very start of the drama. In scene I of the "reading version" Amanda calls Tom and explains, "We can't say grace until you come to the table!" (p. 594). This speech is omitted in the "acting version." Here Amanda opens with a comment on the Northern versus the Southern Episcopalians. She has recently been to church and was refused a seat because a woman told her that the pew was rented (pp. 343–344). Williams has changed an innocent religious activity into a social comment on the North and the state of a church in that area. The rest of this speech is nearly the same, yet Amanda is not as dictatorial in the "acting version." A few lines further, her reaction to Tom's leaving the table is more harsh in the "acting version" than it is in the "reading version." In the "reading version" the passage reads, "[lightly]. Temperament like a Metropolitan star! You're not excused from the table" (p. 594). In the "acting version" it reads, "Temperament like a Metropolitan star! You're not excused from this table" (p. 344). The direction "lightly" is dropped and "the" is changed to the more immediate "this." Thus in the first scene Amanda does not seem to be part of a dream world, but rather a part of a here-and-now world. When Laura offers to get the coffee, Amanda answers:

"No, sister, no, sister—you be the lady this time and I'll be the darky" ("reading version" p. 595). The revised line reads, "No, no, no, no. You sit down. I'm going to be the colored boy today and you're going to be the lady" ("acting version" p. 344). The two important changes in this line are the change from the order "No sister" to the lighter "No, no, no, no," and the use of the more socially acceptable term "colored boy." The next line, "Resume your seat, little sister—I want you to stay fresh and pretty—for the gentlemen callers" ("reading version" p. 595), changes to "Resume your seat. Resume your seat. You keep yourself fresh and pretty for the gentlemen callers" ("acting version" p. 344). Again an order has been changed to a lighter, more conversational command.

In the remainder of scene I only three more changes are of major importance. Amanda again uses colored boy rather than darky. Thus a socially acceptable term is again substituted for a southern one. In the "reading version" a spotlight is placed on Amanda during her speech about her youth and her gentlemen callers. This light is not used in the "acting version," and thus a more realistic, less dreamlike atmosphere is produced. A single spotlight is occasionally used in the "acting version." In this case it is an important omission, for as we have observed, this scene, in the "acting version," seems to bring Amanda into the real world, the world of St. Louis, not the dream world, the world of her youth in the South. The other important change in Amanda, which is noticeable throughout the first scene, is that her speeches are more conversational in the "acting version." She is a participant in the action, and not a dreamy bystander.

In scene II the conversational tone observed in scene I continues to develop in the "acting version." Amanda enters the apartment and finds Laura at the typewriter after learning that Laura has not been attending business school. The "reading version" opens with "Hello, Mother, I was —!" and Amanda replies, "Deception? Deception?" (p. 598). The "acting version" opens with,

> *Laura:* Hello, Mother, I was just.
> *Amanda:* I know. You were just practicing your typing, I suppose.
> *Laura:* Yes.
> *Amanda:* Deception, deception, deception! (p. 346)

In the "acting version" a realistic conversation is created, for Amanda is sure that Laura is deceiving her. In her next speech

Amanda changes "forever" ("reading version" p. 598) to "the rest of my entire life" ("acting version" p. 346), again a more realistic and less dreamlike statement. A more conversational tone has continued to develop when "I thought you were an adult; it seems that I was mistaken" ("reading version" p. 598) is changed to "I was under the impression that you were an adult, but evidently I was very much mistaken" ("acting version" p. 346). This tone is present in many more speeches of scene II in the "acting version." When Amanda tells Laura about her visit to the Rubicam's Business College in the "acting version," we find that Laura really did get sick to her stomach and that the college did call her home "every day," neither of which happens in the "reading version." When Laura starts to play the victrola she is told not to in the "acting version." In the "reading version" she must know she is not to play it by Amanda's facial action. When Amanda asks Laura where she has been going when she should have been at the school, Amanda is much more understanding in the "acting version" than in the "reading version." A few lines further Amanda says, "You did all this to deceive me, just for deception? Why?" ("reading version" p. 600). In the "acting version" three more whys are added, and again the tone is softened. This tone of sympathy, yet more concern, continues. In the "reading version" Amanda says, "So what are we going to do the rest of our lives? Stay home and watch the parades go by?" (p. 600). This is changed to, "So what are we going to do now, honey, the rest of our lives? Just sit down in the house and watch the parades go by." ("acting version" p. 347)

Later in scene II when Laura and Amanda have discussed the boy Laura knew in school, Amanda decides that Laura might marry. Amanda says, "Girls that aren't cut out for business careers usually wind up married to some nice man. Sister, that's just what you'll do!" ("reading version" pp. 601–602). In the "acting version" Amanda explains, "That's all right honey, that's all right. It doesn't matter. Little girls who aren't cut out for business careers sometimes end up married to very nice young men. And I'm just going to see that you do that, too!" (p. 348). The differences in the above speeches again point out, quite well, the differences in the development of Amanda that I have tried to suggest. The "reading version" gives Laura and Tom a stage companion. The "acting version" gives them a mother. Three lines later, the end of scene II, Laura says that she is a cripple. In the "reading version" Amanda's attitude is matter-of-fact. In the "acting version" she is more understanding, more human, more full of and worthy of love. At the beginning of scene III we find Amanda talking on the telephone, attempting to sell magazine subscriptions to lady acquaintances. Money is needed so that she can launch her campaign to obtain a husband for Laura. There are many changes in the conversation between Amanda and Ida Scott. In the "reading version" we find Amanda's speech less emotional and pitiful. She does not receive any sympathy from Ida (p. 603). In the "acting version" Amanda is sweeter, more concerned, more compromising, and thus more hurt when the woman hangs up on her (p. 349–350). These changes can be shown by a look at one line, the last, of this conversation, "I think she's hung up!" ("reading version" p. 603), which is changed to "Why, that woman! Do you know what she did? She hung up on me" ("acting version" pp. 349–350). In the "acting version" we see Amanda as an emotional and thus hurt and insulted individual, not just a line of explanation in a play.

At this point the "reading version" dims out. In the "acting version" we find Amanda giving Tom a health lesson concerning his eyes and posture. After an excess of Amanda's concern, Tom explodes and swears at her. The "reading version" begins action at this point. The difference between the "reading version" and the "acting version" is just a few lines, yet we see another example of Amanda's love and concern for her children, and Tom's reaction to her overbearing love. Also a smooth transition is made from one part of the scene to another without an artificial dimming of the lights.

Tom and Amanda's conversation in scene III includes an argument about a novel. The speeches are not changed importantly. What is important is Tom's reaction. When Amanda calls a novel by D. H. Lawrence "horrible" and something for people with "diseased minds," Tom laughs at her "wildly" and then "still more wildly" ("reading version" p. 604). This is not his reaction in the "acting version," where he merely listens to her speech (p. 350). It is here that we can see the necessity of the additional lines included in scene III, mentioned above. Amanda loves Tom and Tom knows it, and this mutual love is much different from the cold and mocking nature of the characters in the "reading version."

Later in this scene we again find that Amanda's and Tom's lines are more realistic, more emotional, yet more lifelike. When Tom explains that he does not care for his job, Amanda reacts as follows, "What right have you got to jeopardize your job? Jeopardize the security of us all? How do you think we'd manage if you were —" ("reading version" p. 605). In the "acting version" this speech is changed very little, but the changes are important and help explain the change in Amanda. She says, "How dare you jeopardize your job? Jeopardize our security? How do you think we'd manage?" (p. 351). It is now "How dare you" and "our," and the speech is finished and more normal and thus not part of a dream world. As a result of the argument Tom calls Amanda an "ugly-babbling old-witch." He then throws his coat and breaks the glass collection. Laura screams. In the "reading version" we are told "[But Amanda is still stunned and stupefied by the "ugly-witch" so that she barely notices this occurrence. Now she recovers her speech.] [In an awful voice]. I won't speak to you—until you apologize!" (p. 606). What is important here is the use of a written explanation for Amanda's reaction to Tom's insults. In the "acting version" the explanation is omitted. Reaction is expressed, much more naturally, when Amanda says "[in an awful voice]. I'll never speak to you again as long as you live unless you apologize to me" (p. 352). Again Williams has learned to do within the "acting version" of the play that which he had to do outside of the play in the "reading version."

As scene IV opens we find Tom trying to enter the apartment in a state of drunkenness. He drops his key, and Laura lets him in. After a brief discussion about what Tom has been doing, Laura succeeds in persuading him to go to bed. In the "reading version" the scene dims out at this point, and a dreamlike state is again the vehicle for movement from one part of a scene to another. In the "acting version" a more pronounced break is made, for the play moves on to scene V. This is a very slight change, yet a feeling that a real night has passed is created by the scene division in the "acting version." In the "reading version" we are left, and rightly so, with the feeling that this is all part of one action, a feeling that is not the desired reaction in the "acting version."

Amanda has only five more changes in the remainder of scene IV of the "reading version," scene V of the "acting version." The first four changes again show Amanda's lines as more conversational and Amanda as more gentle, more loving and understanding, more realistic. Only one of these changes warrants a close inspection.

Tom has apologized to Amanda, and she "sobbingly" has forgiven him and has explained how much she worries about her children. She has told Tom to try harder, and he says that he does try hard. In the "reading version" Amanda then says:

> [with great enthusiasm]. Try and you will SUCCEED! [the notion makes her breathless]. Why, you—you're just full of natural endowments! Both of my children—they're unusual children! Don't you think I know it? I'm so—proud! Happy and—feel I've—so much to be thankful for but—Promise me one thing, Son! (p. 610)

The above speech seems to be something a mother might say under such circumstances. But note how much more warmly, how much more affectionately, the same lines can be penned:

> [with great enthusiasm]. That's all right! You just keep on trying and you're bound to succeed. Why, you're—you're just full of natural endowments! Both my children are—they're very precious children and I've got an awful lot to be thankful for; you just must promise me one thing. (p. 354)

Amanda's lines in the "reading version" now seem more naturally a part of a Horatio Alger novel or a Dale Carnegie speech. Amanda's lines in the "acting version" are those of a sensitive, frail, emotional woman.

The last change made in scene IV of the "reading version" is at the end. This is a second telephone conversation concerning magazine subscriptions, this time with an Ella Cartwright. There are changes in the first part of the conversation. One finds, again, a more conversational tone to Amanda's language, and she is sweeter and more pitiful in the "acting version." The important change, however, and this change does fit and follow well the changes in tone, appears in the "acting version" as an addition to the conversation. Scene IV of the "reading version" ends with the telephone conversation unfinished. In the "acting version" the call is continued and finished, and in doing so Williams again makes Amanda more human, more sensitive, more pitiful, and more worthy of our sympathy. The end of the conversation is as follows:

> You, you have? You have read it? Well, how do you think it turns out? Oh, no. Bessie Mae Harper never lets you down. Oh, of course we have to have complications. You have to have complications—oh you can't have a story without them—but Bessie Mae Harper always

leaves you with such an uplift—What's the matter, Ella? You sound so mad. Oh, because it's seven o'clock in the morning. Oh, Ella, I forgot that you never got up until nine. I forgot that anybody in the world was allowed to sleep as late as that. I can't say any more than I'm sorry, can I? Oh, you will? You're going to take that subscription from me anyhow? Well, bless you, Ella, bless you, bless you, bless you. (p. 356–357)

Poor Amanda, she so badly wants to sell a subscription, yet she does not remember that all people don't have to "rise and shine" at six o'clock. We can almost see her on her knees, and because her apology is sincere and warrants sympathy she receives it from Ella, and she receives it from us.

From scene V of the "reading version" to scene VI of the "acting version" many minor changes are made in the position of the lines within the scenes and in the meaning of the lines, due to word changes. In the "reading version" the scene opens with Amanda. Ten lines later we find Tom's speech that opens the scene in the "acting version." This rearrangement removes an awkward break in the action of the "reading version" and creates a smoothly moving scene in the "acting version."

In all of the word changes in Amanda's lines, we find her, again, more conversational, more human, and more realistic. It is in this scene that Tom tells her that they shall have a gentleman caller. In the "reading version" Amanda's and Tom's conversation about the caller, Jim, is tight, stiff, unnatural, and unloving—unloving because Amanda reacts very harshly to Tom's withholding of information (pp. 616–621). In the "acting version" Tom and Amanda have a light and fun-filled interplay on the subject of, if, when, and why Jim shall come. Even their discussion of Laura and her handicaps has lost some of its bite (pp. 358–361). Other minor changes are as follows. All of her silver, monogrammed table linen, fresh curtains, a new sofa, and chintz covers ("reading version" pp. 617–618) become three pieces of silver, that old lace tablecloth, no change of curtains, a bright piece of cretonne for the daybed, and a bright cover for the chair ("acting version" p. 359).

Thus we see a more humble and practical Amanda in a more depressing and realistic world. The long-gone father is mentioned several times by Amanda in the "reading version," only once in the "acting version." Again we see Amanda in a less dream-filled world. Near the end of scene V of the "reading version," Tom gets

up to leave and Amanda says, "[sharply]. Where are you going?"
Tom replies he is going to the movies. Amanda's response is critical
("reading version" p. 621). These lines are not included in the
"acting version," and again we see a more understanding, a more
realistic Amanda.

This brings us to the end of Part I in the "reading version." Scenes
VI and VII are located in Part II. This division appears only in the
introductory comment and does not mean a change of acts. Thus
the "reading version," even with a curtain between scenes V and VI,
remains a one-act play. In the "acting version" an act division is
made, and as the curtain rises we look in on act II scene VII.

Scene VII of the "acting version" again presents us with several
examples of tone changes in Amanda's lines. Two examples show
this change in a dramatic manner, for both Laura and Tom have a
new line, a line that is a result of love for and understanding of their
mother. As the scene opens Laura and Amanda are preparing for
the gentleman caller. When Amanda tells Laura she must wear
"Gay Deceivers," she says:

> *Laura:* I won't wear them!
> *Amanda:* You will!
> *Laura:* Why should I?
> *Amanda:* Because to be painfully honest, your chest is flat.
>   ("reading version" p. 623)

Note how this same conversation is changed in the "acting
version."

> *Laura:* I won't wear them!
> *Amanda:* Of course you'll wear them.
> *Laura:* Why should I?
> *Amanda:* Well, to tell you the truth, honey, you're just a
>   little bit flat-chested. ("acting version" p. 363)

We now see Amanda as an understanding, loving mother, this time
in relation to Laura. Amanda then leaves the stage to dress. Her
lines in the "reading version" continue to be harsh and arrogant.
When she comes out with her dress on in the "reading version,"
Laura makes no comment. In the "acting version" the understanding, loving Amanda continues to talk to Laura as she dresses.
When she enters the living room, Laura says "Oh, Mother, how
lovely!" (p. 363).

Later in this scene when Jim has arrived and Amanda comes into the room where Jim and Tom have been talking, Tom makes no comment on her appearance in the "reading version" (p. 630). In scene VII of the "acting version" when Amanda enters, Tom says, "Mother, you look so pretty" (p. 367). These may seem like minor changes, and in the number of words they are. In the overall reaction to and the understood meaning of the play, they are worth paragraphs. In two lines of nine words, Tom and Laura have displayed their love and understanding of Amanda.

As the last scene opens, we see that dinner has been completed. In the "reading version" this is scene VII, in the "acting version" this is act II scene VIII. There is a noticeable difference in Amanda's treatment of Jim in these two versions. Amanda is much less formal in the "acting version." This is suitable to Amanda's new character in the "acting version," for she is now more relaxed with and less formal toward her children and their life. In the "acting version" we find a woman who has accepted more readily her situation in life. The "reading version" is a play that seems to exist in a more dreamlike world. The "acting version" is still a memory play, but it takes place in more realistic surroundings and with more realistic stage devices—the lack of a screen, difference in music, and difference in lighting. Amanda herself has become more realistic. Scene VIII of the "acting version" is a perfect example of this change. In the "reading version" when the lights go out, the conversation is as follows:

> *Amanda:* Where was Moses when the lights went out? Ha-
> Ha-Do you know the answer to that one, Mr. O'Con-
> nor?
> *Jim:* No, Ma'am, what's the answer?
> *Amanda:* In the dark! ("reading version" p. 633)

In the "acting version" the question remains the same. Jim's reply changes to, "No, Ma'am, what's the answer to that one?" Amanda then says, "Well, I heard one answer but it wasn't very nice. I thought you might know another one" (p. 369).

We see Amanda only once more, and this is at the end of the play. There is little change in her lines or in any of the final lines. We discover that Jim is engaged. We see that Tom must leave in the "acting version" as he leaves in the "reading version," and Laura and Amanda are left to fare for themselves. What then is the difference between the 1945 "reading version" and the 1948 "acting version"? The difference is that in the "acting version" we see an understanding and loving mother, we see Amanda as a person who truly suffers, and her suffering is such that others have pity for her. We can see that Laura loves Amanda in the "acting version" for Amanda is not as matter-of-fact toward her problems and her defects. When Laura suffers Amanda suffers also. We know that Tom loves Amanda, for Tom knows that she only wishes him the best. He knows that she is at least trying to understand him and trying to do what is best for Laura, whom he loves so deeply. Therefore, the final scene has changed, for Amanda, Tom, and Laura have all changed. When Tom leaves, we know he leaves a mother that he loves, a mother who loves him. In the "reading version" Tom leaves, and we are glad. In the "acting version" Tom leaves, and we understand, and we are glad, yet we weep, for we know that he would not leave if it were possible for him to stay.

Earlier in this study an opening description of Amanda that is used in the "reading version" was quoted. Now that we have seen how Amanda changes from the "reading" to the "acting version," it is easy to see why this introduction was not included in the "acting version." In the "acting version" Amanda is all that she is supposed to be, for there is much to admire and there is as much to love and pity as there is to laugh at. At times she is tender, at times she is harsh, at times she is foolish. We do not have to be told this in the "acting version." We can see it for ourselves. We can see it in Amanda's lines, lines that are full of life and realism. In the "reading version" Amanda's traits are set forth in the beginning, and as we read the play we think of her in those terms. Thus we see a move from the artificial to the natural, from a weak to a strong Amanda, from a good play to a classic.

As Lester Beaurline explains,[5] the "reading version" should not be reprinted in an anthology, and the "acting version" should not be ignored by a critic. The "acting version" should also not be ignored by the student of drama. Nor should it be ignored by the casual reader, for it is the play, the complete play, *The Glass Menagerie*.

Notes

[1]*Modern Drama,* VIII (September, 1965), 142–143.
[2]The play was not "revised again sometime in the mid-fifties," as Beaurline

suggests. It was revived on November 21, 1956, at the New York City Center. See Signi Lenea Falk, *Tennessee Williams* (Twayne Publishers, New York, 1961), chapter three, note one, for an explanation.

[3]*Op. cit.,* 72–73. George Jean Nathan, *The Theater Book of the Year 1945–1946* (Alfred A. Knopf, New York, 1946), 89–90, clearly shows that it was the "acting version" on stage.

[4]*Modern American Dramas,* edited by Harlan Hatcher (Harcourt, Brace and World's, New York, 1949), 233–274.

[5]*Op. cit.,* 149.

Irony and Distance
in *The Glass Menagerie*

Thomas L. King

Tennessee Williams' *The Glass Menagerie,* though it has achieved a
firmly established position in the canon of American plays, is often
distorted, if not misunderstood, by readers, directors, and audiences. The distortion results from an overemphasis on the scenes
involving Laura and Amanda and their plight, so that the play
becomes a sentimental tract on the trapped misery of two women in
St. Louis. This leads to the neglect of Tom's soliloquies—speeches
that can be ignored or discounted only at great peril, since they
occupy such a prominent position in the play. When not largely
ignored, they are in danger of being treated as nostalgic yearnings
for a former time. But they are not sentimental excursions into the
past, paralleling Amanda's, for while they contain sentiment and
nostalgia, they also evince a pervasive humor and irony and,
indeed, form and contain the entire play.

Judging from the reviews, the distortion of the play began with
the original production. The reviews deal almost wholly with
Laurette Taylor's performance, making Amanda seem to be the
principal character, and nearly ignore the soliloquies.[1] Even the
passage of time has failed to correct this tendency, for many later
writers also force the play out of focus by pushing Amanda
forward.[2] Among the original reviewers, Stark Young was one of the
few who recognized that the play is Tom's when he said: "The
story . . . all happens in the son's mind long afterward. . . ."[3]
He also recognized that the production and Laurette Taylor tended
to obscure the script, for, after a lengthy discussion of Miss Taylor,
he said, "But true as all this may be of Miss Taylor, we must not let
that blind us to the case of the play itself and of the whole occasion."

"Irony and Distance in *The Glass Menagerie*" by Thomas L. King. From the
Educational Theater Journal, 25 (1973), 207–214. Copyright © 1973 by the *Educational
Theater Journal.* Reprinted by permission of the author and the publisher.

Young blamed on Eddie Dowling the failure of the narration noted by others: "He speaks his Narrator scenes plainly and serviceably by which, I think, they are made to seem to be a mistake on the playwright's part, a mistake to include them at all; for they seem extraneous and tiresome in the midst of the play's emotional current. If these speeches were spoken with variety, impulse and intensity . . . the whole thing would be another matter, truly a part of the story." Young indicates that while the reviewers tended to neglect Tom and the soliloquies to concentrate on Laurette Taylor, they were encouraged to do so by a production which made the play Amanda's.

The play, however, is not Amanda's. Amanda is a striking and a powerful character, but the play is Tom's. Tom opens the play and he closes it; he also opens the second act and two further scenes in the first act—his is the first word and the last. Indeed, Amanda, Laura, and the Gentleman Caller do not appear in the play at all as separate characters. In a sense, as Stark Young noted, Tom is the only character in the play, for we see not the characters but Tom's memory of them—Amanda and the rest are merely aspects of Tom's consciousness. Tom's St. Louis is not an objective one, but a solipsist's created by Tom, the artist-magician, and containing Amanda, Laura, and the Gentleman Caller. Tom is the Prospero of *The Glass Menagerie,* and its world is the world of Tom's mind even more than *Death of a Salesman*'s is the world of Willy Loman's mind. The play is warped and distorted when any influence gives Amanda, Laura, or the glass menagerie any undue prominence. If Amanda looms large, she looms large in Tom's mind, not in her own right; though of course the image that finally dominates Tom's mind is that of Laura and the glass menagerie.

The full meaning of the scenes between the soliloquies lies not in themselves alone but also in the commentary provided by Tom standing outside the scenes and speaking with reasonable candor to the audience and reader. Moreover, the comment that the soliloquies makes is not a sentimental one; that is, they are not only expressions of a wistful nostalgia for the lost, doomed world of Amanda, Laura, and the glass menagerie but also contain a good deal of irony and humor which work in the opposite direction. They reveal Tom as an artist figure whose utterances show how the artist creates, using the raw material of his own life.

The nature of the narrator's role as artist figure is indicated by Tom's behavior in the scenes. He protects himself from the savage in-fighting in the apartment by maintaining distance between himself and the pain of the situation through irony. For example, when he gets into a fight with Amanda in the third scene and launches into a long, ironic, and even humorous tirade—about how he "runs a string of cat-houses in the valley," how they call him "Killer, Killer Wingfield," how, on some occasions, he wears green whiskers—the irony is heavy and propels him out of the painful situation, out of the argument, and ultimately to the movies. Significantly, this scene begins with Tom writing, Tom the artist, and in it we see how the artistic sensibility turns a painful situation into "art" by using distance. In his verbal assault on his mother, Tom "creates" Killer Wingfield. Tom's ability to distance his experience, to protect himself from the debilitating atmosphere of the apartment makes him different from Laura. Laura does not have this refuge; she is unable to detach herself completely from the situation and she is destroyed by it. She does, of course, retreat to the glass menagerie and the Victrola, but this is the behavior of a severely disturbed woman. Her method of dealing with the situation, retreating into a "world of her own," does indeed, as Tom says, make her seem "just a little bit peculiar." (scene V).[4] Tom's method is more acceptable; he makes art.

The kind of contrast that exists between Laura and Tom is illustrated by a comment Jung made about James Joyce and his daughter, Lucia. Lucia had had a history of severe mental problems and, in 1934, she was put under the care of Jung. Discussing his patient and her famous father in a letter, Jung wrote: "His [Joyce's] 'psychological' style is definitely schizophrenic, with the difference, however, that the ordinary patient cannot help himself talking and thinking in such a way, while Joyce willed it and moreover developed it with all his creative forces, which incidentally explains why he himself did not go over the border. But his daughter did, because she was not a genius like her father, but merely a victim of her disease." On another occasion Jung said that the father and daughter "were like two people going to the bottom of a river, one falling and the other diving."[5] We see here a psychoanalyst's perception of the problem of artist and nonartist which is much the same as the problem of Tom and Laura. Tennessee Williams' real-life sister, Rose, has also suffered from mental disturbances.

That an author's early play should contain a highly autobiographical character who shows the mechanism by which art is made out of the material of one's life is not particularly surprising, but it is a generally unnoted feature of *The Glass Menagerie* which is inextricably linked to the irony of the soliloquies. For the artist, irony is a device that protects him from the pain of his experience so that he may use it objectively in his art. We may suppose that Swift's irony shielded him from the dark view that he had of the world and that the failure of that irony brought on the madness that affected him at the end of his life. The artist needs his distance from the material of his art so that he may handle it objectively, and the soliloquies of *The Glass Menagerie,* in part, reveal the nature of that distance and how it is maintained.

Generally, each soliloquy oscillates between a sentimental memory of the past, which draws the narrator into it, and a wry irony which keeps him from being fully engulfed and controlled by it. This tension is found in all the soliloquies, though it is not always handled in the same way: sometimes the fond memory is predominant and sometimes the irony, but both are always present. At times, Tom seems almost deliberately to court disaster by creating for himself and the audience a memory so lovely and poignant that the pain of giving it up to return to reality is too much to bear, but return he does with mockery and a kind of wit that interrupts the witchery of memory just short of a withdrawn madness surrounded by soft music and a mind filled with "delicate rainbow colors." In short, Tom toys with the same madness in which his sister Laura is trapped but saves himself with irony.

The opening soliloquy begins on an ironic note. Tom says:

> Yes, I have tricks in my pocket, I have things up my sleeve. But I am the opposite of a stage magician. He gives you illusion that has the appearance of truth. I give you truth in the pleasant disguise of illusion.

These opening lines have a cocky tone—"I will trick you," Tom says, "I'll tell you that I'm going to trick you and I'll still do it even after you've been warned. Besides," he says with perhaps just a touch of derision, "you prefer trickery to the naked truth." Tom begins in the attitude of Whitman on the facing page of the first edition of *Leaves of Grass*—head thrown back, mocking, insolent, but not cruel.

Tom continues in the same mode by saying

> To begin with, I turn back time. I reverse it to that quaint period, the thirties, when the huge middle class of America was matriculating

in a school for the blind. Their eyes had failed them, or they had failed their eyes, and so they were having their fingers pressed forcibly down on the fiery Braille alphabet of a dissolving economy.

In Spain there was revolution. Here there was only shouting and confusion.

In Spain there was Guernica. Here there were disturbances of labor, sometimes pretty violent, in otherwise peaceful cities such as Chicago, Cleveland, Saint Louis . . .

To this point in the speech, Tom's principal mode is ironic, but as he moves on, though the irony remains, a stronger element of sentiment, of poignant memory creeps in. He begins to speak of memory and to enumerate the characters in the play:

The play is memory.

Being a memory play, it is dimly lighted, it is sentimental, it is not realistic.

In memory everything seems to happen to music. That explains the fiddle in the wings.

I am the narrator of the play, and also a character in it.

The other characters are my mother, Amanda, my sister, Laura, and a gentleman caller who appears in the final scenes.

The only break in this poignant mood is the phrase "that explains the fiddle in the wings"—an unfortunate phrase, but demonstrative of the tension, of the rhythmic swing back and forth between sweet nostalgia and bitter irony. The play may be sentimental rather than realistic, but "that explains the fiddle in the wings" breaks the sentiment.

Tom continues by saying:

He [the gentleman caller] is the most realistic character in the play, being an emissary from a world of reality that we were somehow set apart from.

But since I have a poet's weakness for symbols, I am using this character also as a symbol; he is the long delayed but always expected something that we live for.

With these words, the narrator drops his ironic detachment and enters into the mood of memory. The words can hardly be delivered but as in a reverie, in a deep reflection, the voice coming out of a man who, after frankly acknowledging the audience at the beginning of the speech, has now sunk far into himself so that the audience seems to overhear his thoughts. He then shakes off the mood with a return to irony and makes a kind of joke:

There is a fifth character in the play who doesn't appear except in this larger-than-life-size photograph over the mantel.
This is our father who left us a long time ago.
He was a telephone man who fell in love with long distances; he gave up his job with the telephone company and skipped the light fantastic out of town . . .
The last we heard of him was a picture post-card from Mazatlan, on the Pacific coast of Mexico, containing a message of two words— "Hello—Good-bye!" and no address.

There is humor here—not sentiment and not sentimental humor. Tom speaks fondly of his mother and sister and remembers their lost lives and the gentleman caller who symbolizes the loss and the failure, and we can imagine that his gaze becomes distant and withdrawn as he allows himself to be carried away into the memory, but then he remembers another member of the family, the father, and that hurts too much to give in to so he shakes off the reverie and returns once more to irony. The irony is no longer the playful irony of the interlocutor before the audience, but an irony which protects him from the painful memories of the past, that allows him to rise superior to the "father who left us" and to get a laugh from the audience, for the audience should and will chuckle at the end of the opening soliloquy as the light fades on Tom and he leaves his seaman's post. The chuckle may be good-natured, but the humor is not; it is gallows humor in which the condemned man asserts himself before a crowd in relation to which he is horribly disadvantaged by making it laugh. Tom is in control of his memory and already he is beginning to endeavor to work his trick by manipulating the audience's mood.

The opening soliloquy, then, reveals a number of elements that are to be important in the play: it establishes a tension between sentimental nostalgia and detached irony as well as a narrator who is to function as stage magician. The narrator disavows this, but we cannot take him at his word. He says that he is the opposite of a stage magician, but only because his truth looks like illusion rather than the other way round; he is still the magician who creates the play. He says that the play is sentimental rather than realistic, but that is a half truth, for while it contains large doses of sentiment, for the narrator at least, irony sometimes quenches the sentiment. Indeed, Irving Babbit's phrase describing romantic irony is appropriate here: "Hot baths of sentiment . . . followed by cold douches of irony."[6]

he is also set apart

The dominant note of the second soliloquy, at the beginning of the third scene, is irony. In the first soliloquy, Tom has provided the audience with a poignant picture of Laura and Amanda cut off from the world "that we were somehow set apart from." In the second soliloquy, irony almost completely obliterates the poignance as we see Amanda at work trying to find a gentleman caller for Laura, a gentleman caller who is "like some archetype of the universal unconscious." Tom continues the irony as he says:

> She began to take logical steps in the planned direction.
>
> Late that winter and in the early spring—realizing that extra money would be needed to properly feather the nest and plume the bird—she conducted a vigorous campaign on the telephone, roping in subscribers to one of those magazines for matrons called *The Home-maker's Companion*, the type of journal that features the serialized sublimations of ladies of letters who think in terms of delicate cup-like breasts, slim, tapering waists, rich, creamy thighs, eyes like wood-smoke in autumn, fingers that soothe and caress like strains of music, bodies as powerful as Etruscan sculpture.

The mocking humor in this is revealed by the derisive alliteration, the hyperbolic language, and in the humorous, parodying evocation of all the clichés of these stories. The speech makes fun of the literary equivalents of Amanda's memories of gentleman callers in the mythical South. This is not to say that Amanda is savagely attacked with a kind of Swiftian irony; nevertheless, the attack is there, though the irony is balanced somewhat by one irruption of the nostalgic, pitying mode of discourse when Tom says that even when the gentleman caller was not mentioned "his presence hung in mother's preoccupied look and in my sister's frightened, apologetic manner." The irony is also humorous and gets a laugh from audiences if it is performed as irony—especially at the end of the speech where, just as the first soliloquy breaks into a mild humor at the end, Tom humorously parodies the magazine stories.[7]

The first soliloquy strikes a balance between irony and nostalgia, the second is primarily ironic, and the third is primarily nostalgic. The third soliloquy begins with the Paradise Dance Hall:

> Across the alley from us was the Paradise Dance Hall. On evenings in spring the windows and doors were open and the music came outdoors. Sometimes the lights were turned out except for a large glass sphere that hung from the ceiling. It would turn slowly about and filter the dusk with delicate rainbow colors.

Rainbow colors, in fact, fill much of the play: in the scene with
Laura, late at night, after Tom has returned from the movies, the
magic scarf he produces is rainbow-colored—this is one of the few
scenes in which Tom and Laura relate tenderly to one another; the
Paradise Dance Hall filters the dusk with "delicate rainbow colors";
sex hangs "in the gloom like a chandelier" and floods the world
with "brief, deceptive rainbows"; and, in the last soliloquy, Tom
says that he sometimes passes the window of a shop where perfume
is sold—"The window is filled with pieces of colored glass, tiny
transparent bottles in delicate colors like bits of a shattered
rainbow." In the third soliloquy, the Paradise Dance Hall provides
the rainbow colors that fill and transform the alley. The irony
breaks through in only a few places: when Tom disrupts the mood
of magic by pointing out that you could see the young couples
"kissing behind ash-pits and telephone poles," and, as usual, at the
end when he says, "All the world was waiting for bombardments."

All three soliloquies in the first act work together to help define its
movement. The first soliloquy is fairly well balanced between
nostalgia and irony. The detached irony of the second soliloquy
foreshadows Tom's struggle to detach himself from his situation;
after it Tom fights with his mother and leaves to go to the movies.
The third soliloquy asserts the nostalgic mode, and the scene
following this, in which Tom and Amanda talk of the gentleman
caller, is a tender, loving one. We see a playful, warm scene between
Tom and his mother out on the fire escape which shows how, in spite
of their quarrels, Tom and Amanda could also have their warm,
understanding moments. By the end of the first act, the audience
should be taken in by Tom's trick, drawn into the rainbow-colored
world and the pleasant memory of past times. The pain of Tom's
memory has been repudiated in the second soliloquy with irony,
and, after the fight, when Tom runs off to the movies, with the
delicate nostalgia of the third soliloquy, flooding the stage with
rainbow light. The trick is working—we begin to think that Tom
and his mother will get along after all, that a gentleman caller will
come to rescue them, but it remains a trick wrought by the magic of
the rainbow which is broken, whose colors are "deceptive."

The second act begins with a soliloquy which, like the first, strikes
something of a balance between irony and nostalgia. Tom begins
with a description of Jim in language that indicates that he has a
genuine kind of amazed liking for this Irish boy. Only gentle irony
is present in the following words:

In high school, Jim was a hero. He had tremendous Irish good
nature and vitality with the scrubbed and polished look of white
chinaware. He seemed to move in a continual spotlight. He was a
star in basketball, captain of the debating club, president of the
senior class and the glee club, and he sang the male lead in the
annual light operas. He was always running or bounding, never just
walking. He seemed always at the point of defeating the law of
gravity.

Jim is made light of by the phrases "white chinaware"[8] and
"defeating the law of gravity," but the mockery is mild, though it
becomes stronger as the speech continues:

> He was shooting with such velocity through his adolescence that you
> would logically expect him to arrive at nothing short of the White
> House by the time he was thirty. But Jim apparently ran into more
> interference after his graduation from Soldan. His speed had
> definitely slowed. Six years after he left high school he was holding a
> job that wasn't much better than mine.

The irony begins to break through even more strongly after these
words, for Tom was "valuable to him as someone who could
remember his former glory, who had seen him win basketball
games and the silver cup in debating." And the irony even cuts
against Tom: "He knew of my secret practice of retiring to a cabinet
of the wash-room to work on poems whenever business was slack in
the warehouse." A degree of bitterness begins to emerge when Tom
says that, with the example of Jim, the other boys began to smile at
him too, "as people smile at some oddly fashioned dog that trots
across their path at some distance." The bitterness is quickly
moderated, however, when Tom sympathetically remembers his
sister in high school: "In high school Laura was as unobtrusive as
Jim was astonishing." Finally, as always in these soliloquies, the
speech ends with an ironic barb that can often draw a laugh from
the audience. Tom says that when he asked Jim home to dinner "he
grinned and said, 'You know, Shakespeare, I never thought of you
as having folks!' He was about to discover that I did. . . ."

The culmination of all the soliloquies and of the tension between
irony and nostalgia that is carefully developed in them, is in the final
one. Tom's last speech contains just two touches of ironic detachment, but these are critical and are the foci on which this speech
and, indeed, for Tom, the whole play turns. The speech begins with
a touch of ironic humor. In the preceding scene, Amanda has told

Tom to go to the moon. He begins his final speech with "I didn't go
to the moon." This is a decidedly humorous line, indicating that
Tom still has access to his detachment, but the audience is not
laughing anymore, its detachment has been broken down. The
speech then quickly moves into a tone of lyric regret:

> I didn't go to the moon, I went much further—for time is the longest
> distance between two places—
>   Not long after that I was fired for writing a poem on the lid of a
> shoe-box.
>   I left Saint Louis. I descended the steps of this fire-escape for a last
> time and followed, from then on, in my father's footsteps, attempting
> to find in motion what was lost in space—
>   I traveled around a great deal. The cities swept about me like dead
> leaves, leaves that were brightly colored but torn away from the
> branches.
>   I would have stopped, but I was pursued by something.
>   It always came upon me unawares, taking me altogether by
> surprise. Perhaps it was a familiar bit of music. Perhaps it was only a
> piece of transparent glass—
>   Perhaps I am walking along a street at night, in some strange city,
> before I have found companions. I pass the lighted window of a shop
> where perfume is sold. The window is filled with pieces of colored
> glass, tiny transparent bottles in delicate colors, like bits of a
> shattered rainbow.
>   Then all at once my sister touches my shoulder. I turn around and
> look into her eyes . . .
>   Oh, Laura, Laura, I tried to leave you behind me, but I am more
> faithful than I intended to be!
>   I reach for a cigarette, I cross the street, I run into the movies or a
> bar, I buy a drink, I speak to the nearest stranger—anything that can
> blow your candles out!
>   —for nowadays the world is lit by lightning! Blow out your
> candles, Laura—and so good-bye. . . .

The irony in this passage is no longer humorous. When Tom says "I
didn't go to the moon," no one is laughing, and the final, ironic
"and so good-bye" is not even potentially humorous. Tom seems
to have been captured by the memory and the audience has almost
certainly been captured, but Tom, in the end, still has his
detachment. Laura's candles go out and Tom is relieved of his
burden, uttering a final, flip farewell, but the audience has been
more faithful than it intended to be; they are left behind, tricked by

Tom who is free for the moment while they must face their grief, their cruelty, for they are the world that the Wingfields were somehow set apart from, they are the ones who shattered the rainbow.

The soliloquies, then, are of a piece: they all alternate between sentiment and irony, between mockery and nostalgic regret, and they all end with an ironic tag, which, in most cases, is potentially humorous. They show us the artist manipulating his audience, seeming to be manipulated himself to draw them in, but in the end resuming once more his detached stance. When Tom departs, the audience is left with Laura and Amanda alone before the dead, smoking candles, and Tom escapes into his artist's detachment having exorcized the pain with the creation of the play. This is the trick that Tom has in his pocket.

Notes

[1]Lloyd Lewis, describing the Chicago production for the readers of *The New York Times,* Jan. 14, 1945, II, p. 2, said that Eddie Dowling had "brought back Laurette Taylor as a great character actress," called her performance a "tour de force," and, indeed, hardly mentioned anything but her performance in his review. John Mason Brown, when he reviewed the New York production for *The Saturday Review* on April 14, 1945, pp. 34–36, centered on Tom when he summarized the play by speaking of *his* mother, *his* sister, and so forth, but said, "The evening's performance—more accurately the season's—is Miss Taylor's." Joseph Wood Krutch, writing for *The Nation* on April 14, 1945, p. 424, called Amanda the central character: "Laurette Taylor . . . got everything that was to be had from the character of the pitiful and terrible old woman who is the central figure"; he went on to say that the narrator was "usually unnecessary."

[2]Benjamin Nelson, in his *Tennessee Williams: The Man and his Work* (New York, 1961) contributes a twelve-page discussion of *The Glass Menagerie* in which he devotes three short paragraphs to Tom, hardly mentions the soliloquies, and shows his central interest when he says, "Williams' portrait of Amanda is one of the most compelling and honest he has ever drawn" (p. 105). Signi Lenea Falk's slant in *Tennessee Williams* (New York, 1961) is immediately obvious because the discussion of *The Glass Menagerie* appears in a chapter entitled "The Southern Gentlewoman." Esther Merle Jackson, in her *The Broken World of Tennessee Williams* (Madison, Wisconsin, 1966), at least recognizes the importance of Tom as narrator when she says, "Williams creates in this drama a conscious self: the observing and reflecting 'Tom' who projects the flow of experience from his own recall. . . . As the play progresses, it becomes evident that each of the other members of Tom's family represents a position in his pattern of understanding" (p. 86). Esther Jackson, however, is interested only in discussing the fragmentation of consciousness which this represents.

³*The New Republic,* April 16, 1945, p. 505.

⁴Since the pagination differs for different editions of the play, I have identified the passages cited by scene in the text. The passages are taken from the published version rather than the acting version, which differs in some details. I have omitted the stage directions from the citations.

⁵Letter to Patricia Hutchins, cited in Richard Ellman, *James Joyce* (New York, 1959, p. 692). The second quotation is Ellman's paraphrase of a comment by Jung.

⁶Irving Babbit, *Rousseau and Romanticism* (Boston, 1919), Ch. VII.

⁷Paul Bowles' music to accompany this speech indicates how the first production warped the play by throwing all the emphasis on Amanda. His music for Amanda's recollection of her gentleman callers in the first scene is sweet, sentimental, and nostalgic. In this case the music is appropriate; however, the music for this ironic soliloquy continues in the same vein and is patently inappropriate; it seems to force Amanda's wistful vision into a passage which mocks her.

⁸Joseph Wood Krutch completely missed the irony in this passage and in the soliloquies as a whole when he wrote his review for *The Nation,* April 14, 1945, p. 424. He said, "How a man capable of writing as firm as some of that in this play can on other occasions abandon himself to such descriptive passages as that in which a young man is described—in Oscar Wilde's worst style—as 'like white china' is a mystery."

"The play is memory"

Benjamin Nelson

. . . Laura Wingfield, obviously created from the figure of Rose Williams, is the least successful portrait in this play. Too far removed from the world of her brother or mother, she never quite attains a lucid characterization. The girl in glass is a shadow girl whose dilemma motivates much of the thought and action of those around her, but who never emerges as a human being in her own right. She and her plight are too close to the author and rather than probe her experience he makes statements about it. He says, through the characters in his play, that she is beautiful, her beauty and fragility are anachronisms in our world, she will be destroyed, and this is a tragic thing. Rather than cope with her mental unbalance, he creates her with a limp and an inferiority complex to account, at least in part, for her extreme introversion. Otherwise we know very little about Laura, nor are we going to be enlightened during the course of the drama. In a play marked by its objectivity, she remains too subjective. She exists on the single dimension of sympathy.

But if the character of Laura is never fully realized, her plight is given luminous expression. For Williams, the beauty of the ideal is far too delicate to long survive in a world where beauty and delicacy have become little more than petty catchwords. The beauty and gentility of Laura and Rose only make them anachronisms who must either retreat into the ideal beauty of unreality or break in the face of the meaningless harshness of the world outside the glass menagerie. Their plight is symbolized in a poem Williams calls "Lament for the Moths."

A plague has stricken the moths, the moths are dying,
their bodies are flakes of bronze on the carpets lying.
Enemies of the delicate everywhere
have breathed a pestilent mist into the air.

> Lament for the velvety moths, for moths were lovely.
> Often their tender thoughts, for they thought of me,
> eased the neurotic ills that haunt the day.
> Now an invisible evil takes them away.
>
> I move through the shadowy rooms, I cannot be still,
> I must find where the treacherous killer is concealed.
> Feverishly I search and still they fall
> as fragile as ashes broken against a wall.
>
> Now that the plague has taken the moths away,
> who will be cooler than curtains against the day,
> who will come early and softly to ease my lot
> as I move through the shadowy rooms with a troubled heart?
>
> Give them, O mother of moths and mother of men,
> strength to enter the heavy world again,
> for delicate were the moths and badly wanted
> here in a world by mammoth figures haunted![1]

As in *You Touched Me!,* the attempt is made to lead the moth out of her cocoon, into the "heavy world," but this time the attempt is unsuccessful. The moth is much too fragile to fly in "a world by mammoth figures haunted," and the flame of life which glowed with such intensity in the romantic, semi-fantastic figures of Benjamin Murphy and Hadrian, is little more than a flicker in the person of Laura's gentleman caller. . . .

To view Jim's embarrassed confession to Laura as the result of his realization that she may be falling in love with him is to see only one side of the situation. It is true that Jim has unwittingly aroused emotions in Laura with which he cannot cope. But it is similarly true that she has aroused emotions in him which have suddenly upset his life. On the surface Jim is the young man most likely to succeed. He has made the right connections, he is engaged, he is waiting for the inevitable thrust that will catapult him to success. He radiates confidence and his conversation is sprinkled with references to the marvelous opportunities which await the "go-getter." But Jim is not at all as confident as he would have Laura believe. Beneath the bravado and good-hearted bluster, Jim is afraid that democracy— the good old U.S.A.—may leave him behind:

> But just look around you and you will see lots of people as
> disappointed as you are. For instance, I hoped when I was going to
> high school that I would be further along at this time, six years later,
> than I am now—[2]

Although he begins by attempting to convince Laura that she need not feel inferior, he soon betrays his own fear and insecurity. Six years have passed and he is still "planning to get in on the ground floor." Maybe he still will, but after six years with no appreciable progress he must struggle to quell the fear and doubt.

Laura is not the only person "awakened" in their moments together; Jim is awakened to a part of himself that he has not quite successfully suppressed: the unsure, uncertain, frightened Jim O'Connor. His reaction to Laura is that of a bewildered boy, needing tenderness and beauty, and seeing it for a moment in a strange girl. But he cannot accept Laura and preserve his wonderful dream of himself, and she in turn is much too ineffectual to make any positive gesture toward him. So they come together, for one instant, in their mutual need and Jim once more gains control. It's ridiculous, he convinces himself, I must be crazy; I'm engaged to Betty (wholesome part of the American Dream!) and the sooner I tell this odd girl the better. And so he tells Laura and they have suddenly passed in the twilight, each visibly shaken by this unexpected moment of truth.

The story of Laura and Jim is simple and poignant, but it is neither the sole nor the central conflict in the play. Laura's personal dilemma is part of a greater dilemma: the destruction—slow and remorseless—of a family. It is not a melodramatic destruction; there is no battle of angels above them. It is gradual, oblique and laced with pathos and humor, but it is the erosion of a family nonetheless; and the central protagonist of this drama is not Laura, but Amanda, her mother. Amanda Wingfield is

> a litte woman of great but confused vitality clinging frantically to another time and place. Her characterization must be carefully created, not copied from type. She is not paranoiac, but her life is paranoia. There is much to admire in Amanda, and as much to love and pity as there is to laugh at. Certainly she has endurance and a kind of heroism, and though her foolishness makes her unwittingly cruel at times, there is tenderness in her slight person.[3]

Amanda does cling frantically to the past, but she clings just as desperately to the present. She is attempting to hold two worlds together and realizes that both are crumbling beneath her fingers. The world of her youth has already vanished and her constant references to gentleman callers and jonquils are not only out of place in the dingy St. Louis apartment—they are agonizing. Her horribly dated clothing and her mannerisms also underscore her as a foolish old woman impossibly attempting to relive a wasted life. Puritanical and narrow minded, she is appalling in her unreasonable devotion to the past. At the same time she is shrewish, nagging and vulgar in her attempts to cope with the bleak reality of her environment. At one moment she enrages her son with her pretentions and her postures, in the next she prods him and goads him for his inability to be more than a dreamer in a situation where positive action is needed. She berates Tom with the statement that

> you are the only young man that I know who ignores the fact that the future becomes the present, the present the past, and the past turns into everlasting regret if you don't plan for it.[4]

Amanda does not ignore these facts. She recognizes them all too well and attempts to flout them with her own special dreams. She knows that her existence and the existence of her son and daughter is a desperate struggle, and she accepts that struggle. It is this acceptance which elevates her stature above the cloying, often ignorant and embarrassing dowdy, and makes her the most vital and moving character in the play. For whatever Amanda is or does, she possesses a fighting spirit and a stubborn gallantry in the face of overwhelming odds. And in Williams' words, "the most magnificent thing in all human nature is valor—and endurance."[5] It is precisely this heroism and endurance which finally manifest themselves in Amanda and leave us with the impression of a truly valiant woman. This impression does not arise out of any particular word or action. Throughout the play she nags, scolds, dreams, plays the coquette and rages helplessly at her son. And yet, although nothing is said in her behalf, she emerges as a noble and strangely tender figure with a valor that abides alongside pettiness and a tenderness which is at once intertwined with insensitivity and cruelty. It is only at the conclusion when she realizes that her desperate plan for Laura has been crushingly defeated that the great strength and beauty of this woman emerges.

> The interior scene is played as though viewed through soundproof glass. Amanda appears to be making a comforting speech to Laura who is huddled upon the sofa. Now that we cannot hear the mother's voice, her silliness is gone and she has dignity and tragic beauty. Laura's dark hair hides her face until at the end of the speech she lifts it to smile at her mother.[6]

Williams' portrait of Amanda is one of the most compelling and honest he has ever drawn. If it is not a factual likeness of the playwright's mother—he reports that she was aghast when she first viewed Laurette Taylor's performance—it is nevertheless an un-erring emotional portrait drawn with amazing candor and with great objectivity. And the ambivalence in the relationship between the son and the mother is as poignant as it is terrifying.

In his story of the disintegration of a family and the desperate need for one member of that family to break free, Williams has presented a deeply moving play. For Amanda, as for Laura, and even for Jim to a lesser extent, life is finally overwhelming. . . . Tom is caught in the web of his family and is fully aware of his plight. He knows that his job in the shoe company will stifle him and the anguish he feels in the presence of his mother will soon tear him apart. He knows that one day he will have to commit the cruelest act of his life: abandoning mother and sister. As John Gassner has noted, he may love and sympathize with these people but he cannot accept their failure.[7] The world will not accept them and Tom must make his stand in the world, "for nowadays the world is lit by lightning. Blow out your candles, Laura—and so good bye. . . ."[8] So Tom leaves "with a wide-awake attitude toward a society that . . . challenges our intelligence and capacity for action." He cuts the silver cord and like Paul Morel of *Sons and Lovers* walks out of the darkness toward the challenging and shimmering unknown.

But is Tom Wingfield's departure a positive effort on his part, or the final fraying of a bond which could no longer maintain itself? Tom, in the role of Narrator, speaks a good deal about truth and illusion and reality and dreams, but Tom, the protagonist in the story, possesses the romantic soul of a dreamer. Despite the perceptions he shows as Narrator he has as much trouble facing his situation as does his mother. In part, the play is his attempt to overcome his fears, but we are left with no assurance at the conclusion that he has succeeded. He is plainly disgusted with his mother for her poses and apparent refusal to cope with reality, and yet he, too, escapes daily from the oppression of his life by seeking the narcotism of the cinema. Before he makes his final departure Amanda accuses him of living in illusions:

Go to the movies, go! Don't think about us, a mother deserted, an

unmarried sister who's crippled and has no job! Don't let anything
interfere with your selfish pleasure! Just go, go, go—to the movies![9]

Thus a mother who is accused by her son of living in illusions,
makes the most harsh and realistic statement in the play when she
berates the boy, who considers himself the realist, for being an
ineffectual dreamer. The author of the play is here not the narrator.
Williams turns a double-edged blade unmercifully, honestly and
beautifully. When Tom leaves he escapes from a trap, a situation
which is plainly unendurable, but there is nothing heroic or even
positive and challenging in his departure. He is discharged from his
position with the shoe company and he knows he can no longer
remain home. His departure is little more than the snap of a twig in
the wind.

Tom is a part of the dilemma of his family and he cannot break
completely free. If the bond between him and his mother and sister
has frayed, it nevertheless holds and will hold all his life. As he
admits in retrospect, "Oh Laura, Laura, I tried to leave you behind
me, but I am more faithful than I intended to be."[10] Wherever he
may go and whatever he may do, he will always be more faithful
than he intended to be, to Amanda as well as Laura. In the final
analysis, he is the fourth of a quartet caught in the ordinary and
terrifying situation of attempting to exist in a world which gives
them no sensible reason for existence.

The Glass Menagerie exhibits several of Williams' weaknesses as
well as his strengths as a playwright. The great strength of the play is
of course the delicate, sympathetic, yet objective creation of
meaningful people in a meaningful situation. Williams has caught a
decisive and desperate moment in the lives of four individuals and
given it illumination and a sense of deep meaning—no small feat
for any writer.

His characterizations are not equally realized. He has been
unable to create Laura on more than a single dimension, while
Amanda is overwhelming in her multi-faceted delineation. On a
more technical level the play manifests a doubt on the part of its
author toward the power of the written word. As a backdrop for *The
Glass Menagerie,* Williams originally wished to use a screen to register
emotions and present images from the past, present and future. For
example, when Jim O'Connor confesses to the family that he is
going steady with another girl, the legend on the screen is to read,
"THE SKY FALLS." Fortunately, Eddie Dowling deleted these touches

of the poet from his production, but the play still abounds with a number of pretentious statements on the part of Tom as Narrator.

I assume that the final scene between Amanda and Laura is played in pantomime because Williams wished to portray Amanda's dignity through her gestures and her daughter's reaction, rather than through the mother's speech, which during the course of the drama has been either shrill, simpering or saucy. But in relegating this scene to background silence while Tom makes a self-conscious statement about drifting like a dead leaf "attempting to find in motion what was lost in space," he has substituted a painfully pretentious narration for what could have been an intense and luminous moment between the two women.

Again, on the credit side of the author, his play presents genuine situation, motivation and, as Joseph Wood Krutch has noted, "a hard substantial core of shrewd observation and deft, economical characterization." But Mr. Krutch also noted that "this hard core is enveloped in a fuzzy haze of pretentious, sentimental, pseudo-poetic verbiage."[11] In *The Glass Menagerie,* the strained lyricism runs parallel with dialogue that is fresh, alive and highly characteristic, particularly in the speech of Amanda. This dialogue fortunately dominates the proceedings, but the excess of self-conscious "poetical" passages is quite apparent and is a fault of which Williams is to be guilty in much of his later work.

But the great weakness of *The Glass Menagerie* does not lie in its author's artistic or technical deficiencies. The weakness lies at the core of the play and evolves out of what is to become the playwright's hardening philosophical commitment. We can begin to comprehend this when we ask ourselves whether or not *The Glass Menagerie* is a tragedy. It presents a tragic situation and characters who, despite their moodiness and foolishness and self-deception, possess a sense of the tragic. With the possible exception of Laura, they are intensely genuine and the destruction of their dreams and aspirations bears the illusion of great importance. But the play is not a tragedy. The universe of *The Glass Menagerie* does not allow tragedy.

Not one of the characters can cope with his situation. They struggle and their hopes and the destruction of these hopes possess a sense of great importance because Williams has created genuine people in an intensely genuine situation, but they lack the completeness to truly cope with their dilemma. They are not responsible for what has happened to them and they are much too helpless to do more than delay the inevitable. And destruction is inevitable because it is implicit in the universe of Tennessee Williams.

> For the sins of the world are really only its partialities, and these are what sufferings must atone for. . . . The nature of man is full of such makeshift arrangements, devised by himself to cover his incompletion. He feels a part of himself to be like a missing wall or a room left unfurnished and he tries as well as he can to make up for it. The use of imagination, resorting to dreams or the loftier purpose of art, is a mask he devises to cover his incompletion. Or violence such as a war, between two men or among a number of nations, is also a blind and senseless compensation for that which is not yet formed in human nature. Then there is still another compensation. This one is found in the principle of atonement, the surrender of self to violent treatment by others with the idea of thereby cleansing one's self of his guilt.[12]

This statement emanates from the core of Williams' thought and is perhaps his most illuminating commentary about himself and his work. It represents a philosophy, or let us say an attitude toward man in his universe, which is to manifest itself in all his work. It is taken from his short story, "Desire and the Black Masseur," which deals with the final compensation cited in the above quotation: purification through violence. In this tale, a man atones for what the author feels is a cosmic fragmentation and guilt by allowing—and actually furthering—his destruction by a cannibal. In *Battle of Angels* and *The Purification,* we find this same kind of violent cleansing.

The Glass Menagerie is a far cry from any of these works; it is the most non-violent drama written by Williams. Nevertheless it adheres to the belief set forth in the short story. The underlying belief in *The Glass Menagerie* is that there is very little, if any, reason for living. Man is by nature incomplete because his universe is fragmented. There is nothing to be done about this condition because nothing *can* be done about it. Human guilt becomes a corollary of universal guilt and man's life is an atonement for the human condition. In each character in *The Glass Menagerie* there is a part "like a missing wall or a room left unfurnished and he tries as well as he can to make up for it." The mask devised by Laura and Amanda and Tom and Jim is "the use of imagination, resorting to dreams." The Wingfields are broken, fragmented people because "the sins of the world are really only its partialities." They are really not at all responsible for their condition, and thus are in no way able to cope with it. They are trapped in a determined universe. Without some kind of responsibility on the part of the protagonist there is opportunity neither for tragic elevation nor tragic fall. The Wingfields were doomed the moment they were born. At best their struggles will allow them to survive . . . for a time. They will never be allowed to triumph. Thus their struggles, their hopes and even their eventual destruction can never move far beyond pathos. The beauty and magic of *The Glass Menagerie* is that this pathos is genuine, objective and deeply moving.

Notes

[1]Williams, "Lament for the Moths," *In the Winter of Cities,* p. 31.
[2]Williams, *The Glass Menagerie* (New York, 1949), p. 96.
[3]*Ibid.,* p. vii.
[4]*Ibid.,* p. 48.
[5]Williams, quoted in *PM,* May 6, 1945.
[6]Williams, *The Glass Menagerie,* p. 123.
[7]John Gassner, ed., *A Treasury of the Theatre* vol. III, Revised Edition for Colleges (New York, 1951), p. 1033.
[8]Williams, *The Glass Menagerie,* p. 124.
[9]*Ibid.,* p. 122.
[10]*Ibid.,* p. 124.
[11]Joseph Wood Krutch, *The Nation* CLX (April 14, 1945), p. 424.
[12]Williams, "Desire and the Black Masseur," *One Arm and Other Stories* (New York, 1948), p. 85.

Family and Psyche
in *The Glass Menagerie*

Tom Scanlan

Arthur Miller struggled to come to terms with the same family dilemma which O'Neill explored so fully. The American family had failed to achieve its natural harmony, and Miller's reaction was to search the relations between family and society for an answer. Tennessee Williams, too, has reacted to the failed family dream, but in a way opposite to Miller. An inward tendency dominates his dramatic world. He asserts the painful isolation of life against which his characters violently struggle, testing the inner psychological limits of individual existence. O'Neill has rendered this impulse dramatically by trapping the individual within the family, leaving him nowhere else to go, and thrusting him into an iterating cycle of family conflict and destruction. Williams's characters are not trapped in the same way. As in Miller they leave (or are driven out of) the warring family, but the memory of family haunts them relentlessly. Escape from family does not result in a struggle to find a new order to replace family, as in Miller; it means, instead, a desperate search for some anodyne to the pain of being bereft of family.

Rather than Miller's community togetherness or O'Neill's innocent home, Williams's characters will settle for a moment's peace and tenderness. When even that bare victory is not possible, sex and drugs are the (unsatisfactory) substitute. Those who are defeated possess the special sensitivity needed for that contact which allows a brief moment of surcease from the torment of life. But such sensitivity makes them all the more vulnerable. The most intense

"Family and Psyche in *The Glass Menagerie*" (editor's title). From Tom Scanlan, *Family, Drama, and American Dreams* (Westport, Conn.: Greenwood Press, 1978). Copyright © 1978 by Tom Scanlan. Reprinted by permission of the author and the publisher. Pages 156–160 and 166–179, reprinted here, are part of a longer chapter on "Family and Psyche in Tennessee Williams."

expression of their need for love and an end to loneliness is the memory of family, and increasingly Williams's characters settle for transient groupings which are no longer really families at all. If in Williams the ideal of family harmony is reduced to brief gestures of kindness, the family itself is an arena wherein the life forces of sex and fecundity are at war with man's spirit. This would suggest that Williams is dissatisfied with the very conditions of existence (which he symbolizes in family life and family ideal). We can go so far as to say that for Williams the family is the primary expression of organized animal vitality antithetical to the life of the spirit. But we cannot go much beyond this generalization, for Williams does little to define the nature and content of this view. He accepts it rather unselfconsciously with no clear sense of the assumptions it entails. He concentrates, instead, on making the individual's painful relationship to his family vivid and theatrically evocative.

Williams's concern with the interior psychological state repeatedly takes him past the boundaries of the realistic theater which O'Neill accepted in presenting the Tyrone family and which Miller tentatively exploited in the Loman family. His is a drama which, in its emphasis on inner reality, moves further and more consistently than Miller or O'Neill toward the subjective.[1] We have nearly left the domestic drama in talking about Tennessee Williams—nearly, but not quite. For if he moves from realism and from the family, he never quite abandons either. Indeed, part of the peculiarity of effect which Williams achieves depends on the maintenance of those connections. And in tracing their outlines, we are measuring the degree to which the realistic family situation continues to attract our playwrights, even those who are avowedly anti-realistic.

Williams's dramatic vision, as Esther Merle Jackson has usefully pointed out, can be seen to take its cue from the consciousness of one character in each play.[2] Looked at in this way, Williams is projecting a lyric moment of that character which is, for him, the play itself. The technical device Williams uses to justify such an effect—and it is significant here that Williams wants a realistic justification—would be the point of view of a character whose perceptions are not limited in, say, the Jamesian sense, but are distorted through memory, insanity, drugs, alcohol, or dreams. But even while we move into the bizarre or exaggerated situation emblematic of the gauzy mind of the protagonist, we are constantly aware that it approximates a realistic situation.

While Williams's family dramas are consistently more lyrical, looser, and more freewheeling than Miller's, they are not given over to the exploration of psychic irrationality. Nor do they exist primarily on the plan of symbolic abstraction or of idealization. Indeed, the whole matter of distortion—as important as it is to a precise understanding of Williams's tone—can be greatly over-emphasized. Williams's plays, especially those dealing directly with the family, have a concreteness about them which suggests a calculated intensification of realistic conventions rather than a revolutionary break with these customs. Conversational prose speech, coherent and rationalized plot, everyday situations, and understandable motivation are not absent, but rather are slightly stylized to indicate the intense feelings they inadequately represent. Such exaggeration helps to emphasize the cruelty and destruction of family life. The reality of everyday family experience stands behind Williams's plays, and the effect of many of them depends on an audience saturated in realistic domestic drama.[3] . . .

The major dilemmas of family life are imbedded in the dramatic action of Williams's plays, and the ideal that haunts his characters is family-related. Moreover, those plays which have been most successful artistically have been those mostly about the family—the plays up through *Cat on a Hot Tin Roof; Camino Real* is the only exception.

In the earlier plays Williams dramatized the family world in a state of collapse; in later ones family collapse is antecedent to the action. These two situations are combined in *The Glass Menagerie,* Williams's first successful play (and probably his most popular one[4]). The play is a perfect fusion of the two subjects and so is a figure for Williams's entire career. In it the family is long lost and, also, we witness its struggle before it is lost. Williams captures the poignancy of family memories in a way all his own, without sacrificing the core of dramatic conflict which makes such memories less static.

The play is a prime example of Williams's artistry in establishing the relation between his own dramatic world and the conventions of realistic domestic drama to which his audience owes great allegiance, as he well knew. The play occurs in the mind of Tom Wingfield, who drifts in and out of the action both as narrator and participant in a peculiarly appropriate way. From the moment at the beginning when the scrim of the tenement wall dissolves and we enter the Wingfield's apartment, we are reminded of the household of so many family plays. The realistic convention of the fourth wall is evoked as Tom remembers his family.

Tom's evocation is self-conscious, for as "stage manager" he has control over the setting. But Tom is also at the mercy of his memories and irresistibly must relive them. The play keeps us poised between these two styles, these two times, throughout. This is, in fact, its strongest and most subtle conflict. Like Tom, we are continually tempted into the world of a realistic family struggle, but never allowed to enter it completely. The projections and lighting keep the effect slightly stylized during the scenes, the fragmented structure blocks us from too long an absorption in the action, and the reappearance of Tom as narrator forces us back to the present. It is Tom's final reappearance in this role, when the action of the memory play is completed, which releases the tension created between the two styles and dramatizes, in a final rush of emotion, the irretrievable loss of the family which Tom can never escape.

Tom cannot shake the memory of his family from his mind; the dissolution of time and space in the play—that is, in his consciousness—heightens the importance of what he is remembering to make it the most significant thing about his existence. What he remembers—the bulk of the play—centers around two lines of action. The first is his desire to escape from his family just as his father had done before him: "He was a telephone man who fell in love with long distances."[5] Tom, a would-be writer, is caught between a domineering mother and a stultifying warehouse job. He escapes to the porch, to the movies, to the saloon. And finally, in the end, we learn that he has followed his father out into long distances. The second line of action, the principal one, concerns his mother, Amanda, and her attempts to establish some kind of life for Tom's crippled sister, Laura. Amanda pins her hopes on getting "sister" married, after Laura fails because of painful shyness to continue in business school. A "gentleman caller" is found, Jim O'Connor, "an emissary from the world of reality," but all of Amanda's hopes are crushed as he turns out to be already engaged.

The plot is slight stuff, as Williams himself knew.[6] The effect of the play derives in part from the contrast between its two lines of action. Amanda is given over to memories of her past life of happiness as a young southern debutante in Blue Mountain, Mississippi, where on one incredible Sunday she had seventeen gentlemen callers. She imitates the manners and graciousness of those days, a faintly ludicrous parody of southern gentility, the played-out tradition of the antebellum South and its family of security. But she has spirit, too, and responds to the problems of raising two children in a St. Louis tenement during the Depression. Her practicality is what gives her dignity; as she cares for Laura we realize how much Amanda herself needs to be cared for. Her refusal to give in to her nostalgia, even while she indulges in it, enhances her character and makes us susceptible to her longing.

Tom is smothered by such a woman. He fights with her, in part, because she continually tells him what to do: how to eat; how to sleep; how to get ahead. But he fights, also, because her standards represent the conventionality of family responsibility:

> *Amanda:* Where are you going?
> *Tom:* I'm going to the *movies!*
> *Amanda:* I don't believe that lie!
> *[Tom crouches toward her, overtowering her tiny figure. She backs away, gasping.]*
> *Tom:* I'm going to opium dens! Yes, opium dens, dens of vice and criminals, hang-outs, Mother. I've joined the Hogan Gang, I'm a hired assassin, I carry a tommy-gun in a violin case! I run a string of cat-houses in the Valley! They call me Killer, Killer Wingfield, I'm leading a double-life, a simple, honest warehouse worker by day, by night a dynamic *czar* of the *underworld, Mother.* I go to gambling casinos, I spin away fortunes on the roulette table! I wear a patch over one eye and a false mustache, sometimes I put on green whiskers. On those occasions they call me—*El Diablo!* Oh, I could tell you things to make you sleepless! My enemies plan to dynamite this place. They're going to blow us all sky-high some night! I'll be glad, very happy, and so will you! You'll go up, on a broomstick, over Blue Mountain with seventeen gentlemen callers! You ugly—babbling old—*witch.* . . .[7]

He can no more accept her memories of genteel home life in Blue Mountain than he can the spirit with which she has managed to carry on. Both suffocate him. The dead family world of the past is as stultifying as the present. Tom feels the need to escape both:

> You know it don't take much intelligence to get yourself into a nailed-up coffin, Laura. But who in hell ever got himself out of one without removing one nail?
> *[As if in answer, the father's grinning photograph lights up. The scene dims out.]*[8]

The absent father, who still represents the memory of romantic family love to Amanda, is the possibility of romantic escape from family to Tom.[9] He loves his sister Laura, yet he will not accept the responsibility for her which Amanda demands of him. The Wingfields are only a ghost of the family of security, but even this demand to be close-knit repels the restless Tom.

Tom's love for Laura needs to be emphasized, I think, not only because it is one part of the final image of the play—the moment of revelation toward which the action tends—but because it shows Williams's interest in the special qualities of those whom the world has hurt. They are the delicate and fragile people, too sensitive to be able to withstand the crude and harsh necessities by which life drives us along. They have an extraordinary awareness of hidden, almost mystical, qualities of spiritual beauty; and this openness dooms them to be crushed or perverted by the animal vigor of the world.

Laura's specialness is seen largely in contrast with Jim, her gentleman caller. He is, by all odds, the kindest of Williams's emissaries from reality, perhaps because his faith in the American dream of self-improvement and success is so complete as to be itself a touching illusion:

> *Jim [Going after him]:* You know, Shakespeare—I'm going
>   to sell you a bill of goods!
> *Tom:* What goods?
> *Jim:* A course I'm taking.
> *Tom:* Huh?
> *Jim:* In public speaking! You and me, we're not the
>   warehouse type.
> *Tom:* Thanks—that's good news. But what has public
>   speaking got to do with it?
> *Jim:* It fits you for—executive positions!
> *Tom:* Awww.
> *Jim:* I tell you it's done a helluva lot for me.
> *[Image on screen: Executive at his desk.]*[10]

Williams mocks Jim just enough in the use of the slide projection so that we need not take him seriously, yet he makes Jim's naïveté spring from high spirits and an openheartedness which is endearing. He is healthy, happy, and full of hope, but set next to Laura and her needs he is crude, clumsy, and shallow:

> You know what I judge to be the trouble with you?

> Inferiority complex! Know what that is? That's what they
> call it when someone low-rates himself![11]

So much for the intricacies of the human personality. To Jim,
Laura's problems are easily solved and he sets about, in his well-
intentioned way, to cure her. First, he persuades her to dance; and
then, caught up himself in the romance of the moment, he kisses
her. But Laura needs more than a kiss, more in fact than Jim could
ever give her. She needs a tenderness and love that she will never
find. Her needs are so great that to satisfy them would mean altering
the real world to fit her, changing it into a world like that inhabited
by her glass animals, full of delicacy, beauty, and tender harmony.

When this incompatible couple waltzes into the glass menagerie,
they begin to destroy it. At first, Laura does not mind. She is too
thrilled with the prospect of being normal to care whether her glass
unicorn has lost its distinctive horn. But the accident warns us of
what Jim awkwardly confesses after the kiss—that he has made a
mistake and will see her no more:

> I wish that you would—say something.
> *[She bites her lip which was trembling and then bravely smiles. She
> opens her hand again on the broken glass ornament. Then she
> gently takes his hand and raises it level with her own. She carefully
> places the unicorn in the palm of his hand, then pushes his fingers
> closed upon it.]*
> What are you—doing that for? You want me to have
>   him?—Laura?
> *[She nods.]*
> What for?
> *Laura:* A—souvenir. . . .[12]

Laura now knows that she belongs to a different world from Jim. He
wandered into a zoo of exotic animals, but that was on his day off
and he must return to the workaday world.

There will be no normal love of marriage and family for Laura
nor for any of the Wingfields. Laura is too tender, too special, too
fragile like her glass menagerie. It is Tom's painful sensitivity to
Laura's predicament which makes him love her and which drives
him from her. But he cannot escape Laura. The necessity of leaving
her and the guilt over doing so, haunt him:

> Oh, Laura, Laura, I tried to leave you behind me, but I
> am more faithful than I intended to be! I reach for a

> cigarette, I cross the street, I run into the movies or a
> bar, I buy a drink, I speak to the nearest stranger—
> anything that can blow your candles out!
> *[Laura bends over the candles.]*
> For nowadays the world is lit by lightning! Blow out your
> candles, Laura—and so good-bye. . . .
> *[She blows the candles out.]*[13]

Laura's painful encounter with the world's lightning represents all of the Wingfields. Amanda's last glance at her husband's picture reveals as much of her as does Tom's final speech of him. The family is the supreme case of love trying to struggle against the world, and the family fails. Fundamentally romantic, Williams evokes the beauty of failure, the beauty which must fail.

While family life is impossibly difficult, Williams does not actually reject it. Instead, he allows his characters—and his audience—the full "pleasures" of family nostalgia and suffering. It is Williams's peculiar ability to do so without bathos. We can savor the situation because, like Amanda, we are never lost in it uninterruptedly. Williams insures his family memories against outright sentimentality by a delightful (and convenient) comic touch. He does not really create a comic perspective, which would change the meaning of his vision and would suggest the sanity of compromise. Rather, he edges the serious matter of his plays with humor. For example, early in *Orpheus Descending* one of the minor characters declares that most people find hate in marriage and an outlet in money. Her laughter at this observation is a perfect Williams moment. It conveys his temporary emotional defense against the painful truth. *Streetcar* is framed in the same way, with a dirty joke at the beginning and an ironic double entendre at the end: "This game is seven-card stud." Williams seldom maintains his comic view, however, since it is for him, and for his strongest characters, a temporary way of keeping the world at bay. When he waxes "true," his characters speak directly, often lyrically, and the ironic edge disappears. Maggie, in *Cat,* has this edge, this style as part of her character. For her, it is a defense against the suffocating world of her in-laws. At private moments she may drop this defense; the curtain parts, and we see the loneliness, the isolation, and the gentleness within her. The painful inner lives of his characters remain as desperate as ever, only we are given alternate moments of rest from the hurt.

The distancing in *The Glass Menagerie* is fully and artfully done. In Tom's opening speech, for example, the touch of social comment which appears mocks the world of the middle class as well as itself:

> In Spain there was revolution. Here there was only shouting and confusion. . . . This is the social background of the play.[14]

Later, when this motif reappears, it is directly associated with the dilemmas of the Wingfield family. Their private world looks out on the social world in the same way that their windows look out on the alley. Tom says to the audience:

> Couples would come outside, to the relative privacy of the alley. You could see them kissing behind ash-pits and telephone poles. This was the compensation for lives that passed like mine, without any change or adventure. . . .
>   In Spain there was Guernica![15]

And immediately Amanda unwittingly provides the mocking counterpoint:

> A fire-escape landing's a poor excuse for a porch.
> *[She spreads a newspaper on a step and sits down, gracefully and demurely as if she were settling into a swing on a Mississippi veranda.]* What are you looking at?[16]

A more often used technique in *The Glass Menagerie* to provide a comic edge is the projection of legends or images onto a wall in the Wingfield apartment, an element which is frequently dropped in production.[17] The published editions of the play continue to retain them. Williams argues that their use is important to maintain a sense of the play's structure beneath its episodic surface.[18] A number of the projections do seem to have only this architectural function: legends such as "After the Fiasco," "You Think I'm in Love with Continental Shoemaker's?," "High School Hero;" images such as typewriters or a wintry scene in the park. But many are obviously funny, sardonic, or ironic as well. Amanda's memories of Blue Mountain are introduced with "Ou Sont Les Neiges d'Antan?" Tom's desire for adventure brings forth the image of a sailing vessel with a Jolly Roger. Music, too, is used to evoke straightforward emotion. "Between each episode it [the theme tune] returns as a reference to the emotion, nostalgia, which is the first condition of the play."[19] But music also mocks the characters as

when Amanda's self-pitying reproach to Tom's rudeness is introduced with "Ave Maria."

Perhaps the most complex use of these alternating effects is near
the end of the play. Laura and Jim waltz to "La Golondrina." Their
kiss is preceded by the symbol of Laura's freakish beauty—a
projected image of blue roses—and swelling music. Then, having
given us the emotional luxury of this melodrama, the legend
becomes slightly ambiguous—"Souvenir" anticipates the broken
glass figure Laura will give to Jim, and it also comes directly after the
kiss and may refer to it as well. There is less doubt about the next
legend. Jim's cliché explanation of his feelings for another girl
brings forth the mock-enthusiastic "Love!" on the screen, and
Laura's tender gesture with the broken unicorn ends with a choice
of the legend "Things Have a Way of Turning Out so Badly" or the
harsh image "Gentleman Caller Waving Good-bye—Gaily." Finally,
when Jim tells Amanda he is engaged to another girl, we read the
sardonic "The Sky Falls."

Williams tries to have his sentiment and mock it, too, using these
devices both to intensify the family drama and to pull back from it.
These "plastic" elements, then, are Williams's way of using the
realistic situation while not being exclusively bound to it. The core
of the play is the attempt by Amanda to find a family and the desire
by Tom to escape from family. This surface action is alternately
heightened and diminished by these nonrealistic devices. We are
asked to embrace the characters and to laugh at them, to empathize
and then to sympathize. Much of the same strategy can be seen in
the dialogue, once we are alerted to it. Amanda's telephone
campaign to sell subscriptions to the magazine *Companion* is filled
with this juxtaposition of tears and laughter. More poignantly, her
memories of her home life in Blue Mountain are made up of a
dramatic alternation between vivid nostalgia and shrewd practicality:

> Finally there were no more vases to hold them, every available
> space was filled with jonquils. No vases to hold them? All right,
> I'll hold them myself! And then I—*[She stops in front of the picture.
> Music plays.]* met your father! Malaria fever and jonquils and
> then—this—boy. . . . *[She switches on the rose-colored lamp.]*
> I hope they get here before it starts to rain.[20]

Nearly lost in the intensity of her memory, Amanda begins to
speak as though the past were the present, only to be brought up
short by the reality of her situation. The rose-colored lamp is both a

reprise of her vulnerability to charm and an instance of her coping, in the only way she knows how, with the situation in which that vulnerability has placed her: she puts a good light on harsh truths, and she dresses up the faded room to catch the gentleman caller for sister. And one might even say that all the Wingfields get caught out in the rain, away from the warm safety of home. Thus, the drama is embodied in the rhetoric and through its sequential movement each emotionally resonant element is followed by a flat deflation.

Williams uses a similar technique to add a more complex texture to the raw emotions of the Wingfields' family battles. Tom's angry speech denouncing his mother as a witch is slightly muted by his satiric, fanciful tone. But if the direct emotion is reduced in volume, it can also be said that the sense of calculation which Tom's imagery implies makes the hurt Amanda receives all the keener for having been so carefully designed. And in the rare moments when mother and son can talk to, rather than at, each other, Williams manages this shift in tone with greatest delicacy:

> *Amanda:* When I was a girl in Blue Mountain and it was
> suspected that a young man drank, the girl whose
> attentions he had been receiving, if any girl *was*, would
> sometimes speak to the minister of his church, or
> rather her father would if her father was living, and
> sort of feel him out on the young man's character.
> That is the way such things are discreetly handled to
> keep a young woman from making a tragic mistake!
> *Tom:* Then how did you happen to make a tragic mistake?
> *Amanda:* That innocent look of your father's had every-
> one fooled! He *smiled*—the world was *enchanted*! No
> girl can do worse than put herself at the mercy of a
> handsome appearance! I hope that Mr. O'Connor is
> not too good-looking.
> *Tom:* No, he's not too good-looking. He's covered with
> freckles and hasn't too much of a nose.
> *Amanda:* He's not right-down homely, though?
> *Tom:* Not right-down homely. Just medium homely, I'd
> say.[21]

The lines play first between Amanda's nostalgia and Tom's blunt irony, and then between her ecstatic memories (with the painful lesson they teach) and Tom's more gentle teasing. At moments such as these, the play's tone becomes a mode of encounter between characters, its surface ingenuity a way of revealing inner lives. The

Wingfields exist most vividly when they appear to us caught between moments of direct revelation of their psyches and moments of indirect relief from that painful confrontation. In *The Glass Menagerie* the longing for the family of security is mocked but never abandoned, indulged even as it is shown up.

In *The Glass Menagerie* Williams consciously manipulated his subject matter and his tone, playing off the oppressiveness of the family of security against a teasing stylized realism. He did not grapple with the assumptions beneath the conflicting claims of personal freedom and security, nor did he construct a dramatic action which defined them. Rather, he relied on the evocative power of family strife, running the risk of being merely agitated and pathos-filled as in the soap opera. His family victims are at their most vivid at those points where they are both caught up in their lyrical self-indulgence and at the same time aware of the difficulty in communicating to those around them what they truly feel.

Williams does not test the family attitudes which are his subject. He has evoked family fears and frustrations without probing them. But it is important to recognize the genuine, if limited, appeal of Williams's strategy. He has asked us to see his plays as artifice and as reports on reality. And he has used the artificial, "plastic" elements both to intensify and to relieve the intensity of the family struggles. This paradox is a most intriguing one. He has counted on our familiarity with the family drama, reminded us of it, and then eluded its more rigid restrictions. He has been a realist, if only in part, to refresh our response to the dilemmas of family life. His best plays remind us of our quest for relatedness and independence and so depend on, and contribute to, the very tradition of American domestic drama which he proposed to escape.

Notes

[1]For an extended analysis of American drama in terms of its expressionist elements, see Louis Broussard, *American Drama: Contemporary Allegory from Eugene O'Neill to Tennessee Williams* (Norman, Okla., 1962).

[2]Esther Merle Jackson, *The Broken World of Tennessee Williams* (Madison, Wis., 1965), pp. 26–42.

[3]Jackson's book, the most suggestive and insightful yet done on Williams, argues the opposite point: Williams is an anti-realist whose work embodies—at one point she says it inaugurates—a third phase in the development of modern, expressionist form. *Ibid.*, pp. viii, 20–42.

[4]Jackson, *Broken World,* p. viii, note 1.
[5]Williams, *The Glass Menagerie* in *The Theatre of Tennessee Williams,* I (New York, 1971), p. 145.
[6]"A free, imaginative use of light can be of enormous value in giving a mobile, plastic quality to plays of a more or less static nature." Williams, "Production Notes," *Menagerie,* p. 134.
[7]*Ibid.,* pp. 163–164.
[8]*Ibid.,* pp. 167–168.
[9]Nancy M. Tischler, *Tennessee Williams: Rebellious Puritan* (New York, 1961), p. 97.
[10]Williams, *Menagerie,* p. 199.
[11]*Ibid.,* p. 220.
[12]*Ibid.,* pp. 230–231.
[13]*Ibid.,* p. 237.
[14]*Ibid.,* p. 145.
[15]*Ibid.,* p. 179.
[16]*Ibid.,* p. 180.
[17]The original New York production and the recent revival [1975] both omitted the projections. Without them the play is moved even closer to the conventional realism of domestic drama, a tendency which can also be seen in the Broadway productions of *Streetcar,* which have deemphasized the expressionist elements in such scenes as those presenting symbolic images of Blanche's mental state.
[18]Williams, "Production Notes," p. 132.
[19]*Ibid.,* p. 133.
[20]*Ibid.,* p. 194.
[21]*Ibid.,* p. 186.

The Sister Figure
in the Plays of
Tennessee Williams

John Strother Clayton

He runs incessantly about the streets and seeks—the sister.
Wilhelm Stekel

*Oh, Laura, Laura, I tried to leave you behind me, but I am
more faithful than I intended to be!*
Tom Wingfield
The Glass Menagerie

. . . The central element of Williams' past, as he presents it to us in
his fiction, is his sister, a sister who became for him the only person
in the world who accepted him without reservation, who shared his
secret world with him, who loved him, and whom he loved with all
the emotional intensity of a deeply sensitive and lonely child. For
Williams, as he presents himself in his writing, was both. In his
writing it is painfully clear that he lives with his nerve endings raw
and exposed, hypersensitively aware of all that impinges upon the
senses: sounds, odors, colors, images—only the sense of taste (in
the literal meaning of the word) seems to be absent in his vivid
awareness of the world about him. To some the "thousand natural
shocks that flesh is heir to" hardens the metal of their being,
tempers the steel; others, experiencing the same or similar traumas,
soften so that the slightest pressure leaves its impression for a
lifetime. The new boy in every neighborhood in the country is
challenged by the local Tom Sawyer, or as in *Rebel Without a Cause*,
forced to prove his manhood in a "chicken run" held by the
neighborhood gang. The town hellion who is the minister's son is

part of our folklore; the competition between father and son a staple of popular television and screen fare. The ninety-seven pound weakling who, having been bullied on the beach, realizes his fantasies by himself becoming a bully on the beach has produced untold scores of muscle builders with similar ambitions.

Tennessee Williams remained the physically delicate child who did not send away for the barbells, the bullied son who did not fetch Pap a clout alongside the head and escape on a Mississippi raft, the new boy who stayed home when the "chicken-run" was held, and the minister's (grand)son who delayed becoming a hellion until he was old enough to vote.

He stayed at home with his sister. And her love for him and his love for her was the only strength and escape and rebellion that he knew—until he began to write.

The sister appears most clearly in the short "Portrait of a Girl in Glass," the sketch which was later realized as the poignant memory play, *The Glass Menagerie,* and in the clinical detailed, sensitively written case history of his childhood, "The Resemblance Between a Violin Case and a Coffin," first published in *Flair Magazine* in 1950. In the latter story Williams describes the painful experience of the break-up of the companionship with his sister to which he so desperately clung as a substitute for the other relationships normal to childhood. His situation, evidently, did not go unnoticed by his family. "They were continually asking me why I did not make friends with other children," he writes. "I was ashamed to tell them that other children frightened me. . . ." As for the sister, her "wild imagination and inexhaustible spirit made all other substitute companions seem like the shadows of shades. . . ."

In "The Resemblance Between a Violin Case and a Coffin" we meet most of the elements that will be with us again and again in his work: the seldom present father, "whom I should say, in passage, was a devilish man, possibly not understood but certainly hard to live with," out on the road with his sample case on long trips; the homosexual attachment for the handsome Richard Miles whom "I resented . . . fiercely even though I began, almost immediately after learning of his existence, to dream about him as I had formerly dreamed of storybook heroes;" the developing sense of guilt as "I had begun to associate the sensual with the impure, an error that tortured me during and after pubescence;" and the displaced incest-love, "The transference of my interest to Richard now seemed complete. I would barely notice my sister. . . ."

The progression Williams describes is quite clear. He and his sister enjoy a separate world together. His sister reaches puberty, develops mysterious symptoms, and is treated with new gravity and deference by the mother and grandmother. "In this way was instituted the time of estrangement that I could not understand. From that time on the division between us was ever more clearly established." And, as the basis for deep antagonism, "It seemed that my mother and grandmother were approving and conspiring to increase it." Now, almost overnight, his sister's long copper curls are removed, the costume changed, and "I noted . . . she had now begun to imitate the walk of grown ladies, the graceful and quick and decorous steps of my mother. . . ."

"For the first time, yes, I saw her beauty. I consciously avowed it to myself, although it seems to me that I turned away from it, averted my look from the pride with which she strolled into the parlor and stood by the mantel mirror to be admired. And it was then, about that time, that I began to find life unsatisfactory as an explanation of itself and was forced to adopt the method of the artist of not explaining but putting the blocks together in some other way that seems more significant to him. Which is a rather fancy way of saying I started writing. . . . "

And now, into the scene, comes the young and handsome Richard Miles, carrying his violin case for he is to play in a duet with the sister, who plays the piano. Together, they must rehearse, and, naturally, the sister experiences her first true love. It is a wretched experience, for it turns her into an idiot at the keyboard, forgetting passages of music, making clumsy mistakes, feeling the despair of appearing a fool in the eyes of someone she worships with all the power of adolescence. The best that can be said about the situation is that Richard is kind, helping her through the tough passages, encouraging her when she despairs. To all of this, the young author is a silent and absorbed witness. At first he watches in bitter jealousy this warm relationship with the only person who belongs to him. But as he watches their young and innocent relationship develop, a strange thing happens; he finds himself erotically stimulated by the sight of their rehearsal together. Can it be that Richard is all that he longs to be? Handsome, talented, the love object of his sister? No, of course that is not it. He does not wish to *be* Richard. Such are not his fantasies. Nor does he wish to *love* his sister. That would never do. If he is stimulated by the sight, it cannot be because he loves the sister, it must be because he loves Richard. Of course. And so, "The transference of my interest to Richard now seemed complete. I would barely notice my sister. . . ." Serve her right too. Teach her to desert him!

Is this the answer to the story he tells? Possibly. I do not know. Speculation is inevitable. In any event his fantasy world is now built upon homosexual daydreams involving Richard, and, on one occasion, as he watches a gentle embrace pass between them when his sister has become upset over her repeated failures at the piano, "my body learned, at least three years too early, the fierceness and fire of the will of life to transcend the single body, and so to continue to follow light's curve and time's. . . ." And of course, the feeling of guilt as he says to himself "Yes, Tom, you're a monster!"

In the story "Portrait of a Girl in Glass" we come to know the sister better—the sister as she will appear to us later in *The Glass Menagerie* and as her ghost will appear in many other ladies to come. Here the locale is part of the new and difficult period of Williams' life, when his family had moved to St. Louis where he was to experience the horror of "a small wage earner in a hopelessly routine job," where he was to learn what it meant to be among the have-nots and so regarded, and where he was to live amid bleak surroundings, watching the slow deterioration of his sister which was eventually to lead her to a mental institution. It is here in this drab depression home that we first meet "Laura," who "made no positive motion toward the world but stood at the edge of the water, so to speak, with feet that anticipated too much cold to move."

It is in this story that Williams gives us an early glimpse of his great talent for effectively utilizing concrete surroundings for both their dramatic and symbolic value. The alley below the sister's room is called Death Valley because in it cats are trapped by a "particularly vicious dirty white Chow who stalked them continually." From this world, Laura retreats. "The areaway had grown to be hateful to Laura because she could not look out on it without recalling the screams and the snarls of killing. She kept the shades drawn down, and . . . her days were spent almost in perpetual twilight." Within this setting, Williams evokes a memorable image, "The charm of the room was produced by his sister's collection of glass. . . . When you entered the room there was always this soft, transparent radiance in it which came from the glass absorbing whatever faint light came through the shades on Death Valley."

The girl who had been his alter ego as a child, whose fingers had stumbled over the keys in the presence of a handsome lad, is now too shy and withdrawn to face the world. To her, Williams gives three avenues of escape from reality: her animals, her records, and a book.

The animals provide her with a fantasy world and fantasy companionship; the records take her back into the past. "Laura seldom cared for these new records, maybe because they reminded her too much of the noisy tragedies in Death Valley or the speed-drills at the business college. The tunes she loved were the ones she had always heard." From the book, *Freckles,* by Gene Stratton Porter, Laura is provided with a "phantom lover." According to Williams, Freckles, "a one-armed orphan youth who worked in a lumber-camp, was someone that she invited into her bedroom now and then for a friendly visit. . . ." These avenues— the past, fantasy, the phantom lover—will all appear again.

The Laura of "Portrait of a Girl in Glass" is essentially the same person when she reappears in *The Glass Menagerie,* though she has been deprived of her phantom lover. She has been compensated for this loss, however, by the addition of a physical flaw—a device that Williams will utilize frequently throughout his work—both to represent and to account for the flawed nature of her character. It is an outward and visible sign of an inward and spiritual flaw.

When we next see the sister, a considerable change has taken place, though the family group remains the same: mother, sister, brother, and absent father. They appear in another of Williams' memory plays, *The Long Goodbye,* which deals with a young Depression writer during the early days of the Roosevelt administration. He alone remains in the apartment once occupied by his family, and he, too, is moving on. As workmen remove the contents of the apartment, various elements evoke memories from the past, some of which are dramatized while others are narrated. The theme of the play is stated in a conversation between brother, Joe, and a companion, Silva:

> *Silva:* Goodbye? 'S not in my vocabulary! Hello's the word nowadays.
> *Joe:* You're kidding yourself. You're saying goodbye all the time, every minute you live. Because that's what life is, just a long, long goodbye! To one thing after another! Till you get to the last one, Silva, and that's— goodbye to yourself!

During the "flashbacks" we see the gradual estrangement between Joe and his sister, Myra. Joe is jealous and suspicious of the girl's suitors, accuses her of cheap conduct, and triumphantly confronts her with the evidence of premeditation—a contraceptive—dropped by one of her callers. . . . That Joe is more than justified in his suspicions is possible, indeed probable, as Myra infinitely prefers the escape she has chosen to the deadly, poverty-ridden life of a shop girl. So the sister who goes out with other men disappears from his life, looking like a whore—"like a cheap one, Myra, one he could get for six!" And the brother is left alone.

Of course another kind of ending to the story is possible. The sister need not desert the brother. Indeed if one may dream—and why not?—the brother can possess the sister. It is a dangerous thought, a guilty thought, a thought that should be hidden. But it is a consummation devoutly to be wished by the brother figure in Williams' works.

The wish is fulfilled, interestingly enough, in the only verse-drama that Williams has published, *The Purification,* a symbolic fantasy more or less located in a country similar to that found around Taos, New Mexico, which on the surface seems to tell of a murder investigation-trial conducted along ritualistic lines. The characters are Spanish ranchers and Indians. The family group consists of the father, mother, brother, and sister. It appears that a young girl (the sister) has been murdered, and in the course of the investigation it is revealed that she had married a former repairman who is now a rancher. Their union was never consummated. She has had an incestuous relationship with her brother which has led the rancher-husband to kill her with an axe when he finds them together. The play concludes with the suicide of the brother and the husband.

While *The Purification* is doubtless one of Williams' minor efforts, it is nevertheless a crucial play for the student of his writing. Unfortunately, a detailed examination of the elements that appear in *The Purification* necessitates a more liberal reference to the body of Tennessee Williams' work than the length of this article permits. In addition, much of the material is too clinical for general interest. It is sufficient to note that in *The Purification* the brother possesses the sister, but the price is heavy: disgrace for the family, death for the sister, guilt and death for the brother. But must the conclusion reached in *The Purification*—guilt and atonement—be the penalty? Is it possible for brother and sister to remain together, even to marry? Can it possibly be arranged for them to live free from guilt happily ever after? With a little ingenuity, it can.

To accomplish this purpose, Williams (with a young collabora-
tor, Donald Windham) chose to adapt a short story by D. H.
Lawrence entitled "You Touched Me," which is included in a
Lawrence collection, *England My England and Other Stories* (New York,
1922), pp. 147–171. The changes made by Williams in adapting the
Lawrence story are striking as he changes the pattern to conform to
the family situation of Mother, Father, Sister, and Brother. The
treatment of the sister figure will serve as an example of the
transformation. In order to illustrate this, a few details from the D.
H. Lawrence story need to be mentioned. As written by Lawrence,
"You Touched Me" deals with the Rockley sisters, Matilda and
Emmie, who live in an ugly, brick house amid a now abandoned
pottery which has been "permanently shut." At the beginning of
the story Matilda and Emmie are already "old maids," though
Matilda is only thirty-two, while her sister is two years younger.
Matilda is described as "a tall, thin, graceful girl, with a rather large
nose," while Emmie is shorter and plumper and looks up to her
older sister "whose mind was naturally refined and sensible."
When the girls were in their teens, Ted Rockley, the father, having
had four daughters and no sons, adopted a boy of six from a
London charity institution. The boy's name is Hadrian. He is never
really accepted by the sisters and eventually runs away, making his
living in Canada, fights in World War I, and returns to the Rockley
home on leave after the war. Hadrian, now twenty-one, proposes
marriage to the thirty-two year old Matilda. Matilda refuses. The
father changes his will to read that if she refuses his request, the
entire estate will go to Hadrian. As the father is dying, Matilda
decides to marry Hadrian.

As adapted for the stage by Williams (with Donald Windham) the
play *You Touched Me!* has a number of suggestive changes. The thirty-
two year old Matilda of the large nose has somehow changed to
"Matilda is at the tea-table polishing silver and washing little glass
ornaments. She is a girl of twenty and has the delicate, almost
transparent quality of glass." Matilda is portrayed as "dreamy," not
taking part in the conversation when the minister calls, and—when
Hadrian is expected home—she says, "I won't stay. I can't stay. I'll
take a trip somewhere . . . I feel unbearably self-conscious with
him around. I couldn't speak to him in a natural voice."

This reaction is identical to the one experienced by Tom in "The
Resemblance Between a Violin Case and a Coffin." Secretly
attracted to Richard Miles, Tom flees in his presence. ". . . I did a

thing so grotesque that I could never afterward be near him without a blistering sense of shame. Instead of taking the hand, I ducked away from him . . . and fled into a drugstore just beyond." And again, "I never knew when the front door might open on Richard's dreadful beauty and his greeting which I could not respond to, could not endure, must fly grotesquely away from." This reaction formation will be a characteristic of many of Williams' characters (notably, Miss Collins in *Portrait of a Madonna,* who, interestingly enough, also flees from a handsome man she loves named Richard). "Why are you running away?" asks Emmie of Matilda in *You Touched Me!*

There is more than a suggestion in the play that the Captain has adopted his own illegitimate child in Hadrian. When Hadrian announces to the Captain that he has found a woman, the Captain is unable to imagine who it could be—guesses it to be Phoebe, the buxom, comic maid.

> *Hadrian:* No, not Phoebe.
> *Captain:* Who, then?
> *Hadrian:* Matilda!
> *Captain: (Suddenly grave.)* What? Your sister?
> *Hadrian:* She isn't my sister. We're not blood relations.

The fantasy is complete. It is all right for Hadrian, because of course they are not really blood relations—or are they?

> *Captain:* Hadrian is my son.
> *Emmie:* Matilda is your daughter. Are you—mad?

Mad or sane, the father approves the wedding, and—as Hadrian observes—"Why shouldn't she want me? I'm lonely and looking about for love—and so is she." The only problem that remains is to realize physically what intellectually has been rationalized as acceptable. What will the relationship be? Hadrian speaks to Matilda:

> Why nothing in the world is as gentle as you are. You're as delicately put together as—one of those misty little white cottony things that float around in the sunlight, scarcely seeable, they are so fine and soft. Touch them? You wouldn't dare. It's almost too much to look at them. When I escaped from the prison camp, I had to stick a knife in a guard. As he went down, I saw he was only a kid and just as—gentle—as you are. The life in him yielded as softly as tissue paper. I knew very well that gentle things, such as that boy and you, are made to be gently treated.

Barely touched, hardly breathed upon. Look! *(She looks at his outstretched hand.)* Do these impress you as being dangerous fingers? Do they look to be fierce and cruel? They're not. They wouldn't dare touch you without your permission. And if they did, having secured your permission, they'd do it so lightly, with such respect that they'd draw back the moment they moved forward. They'd be more frightened than you are of using too much pressure—of bruising—or leaving the tiniest scar. I'm a gentle person.

In this passage we have an example of lines that have a clearcut stage value, while containing a number of other insights available to the reader. The stage value is, of course, the kindness of the hero, Hadrian, as he gently approaches the frightened, over-shy Matilda —soothing her, reassuring her. Beyond that, however, are clearly embedded the themes of incest and guilt.

Here we find the desire for the sister, the gentle hands (even with permission!) "draw back the moment they move forward." Here too the sister is portrayed—not as she is by D. H. Lawrence—but as the sister image we have met: delicate, shy, loved by the brother who is more frightened (and guilty) of leaving the tiniest scar than she is. It is also possible to find in the escape from prison fantasy (which does not appear in the Lawrence story) the symbolic account of the brother figure's own escape from the prison of his home—an escape which necessitated (as he testifies in the *The Glass Menagerie*) cruelty toward the guard, i.e., the mother who held him in prison. This is not to suggest that such symbolism (if it exists at all) is intentional, nor, again, of immediate value in stage interpretation. In reviewing Williams' total work, however, it is difficult not to reach some such conclusion as is suggested above.

Matilda is strongly attracted to Hadrian—as he is to her—but she is too shy to reveal it. As soon as Hadrian appears, Matilda announces a fictitious trip that she is taking that evening. Throughout the play she is portrayed as afraid of life, as she has always been:

> *Hadrian:* You were afraid of everything in those days.
> *Matilda:* I still am.

But when the chips are down, it is Hadrian, the brother, who is unable to make the final, physical move. Urged by the Captain-Father that the only way to win her is to "grab her," Hadrian girds up his loins for the attempt, but at the last moment his nerve fails. It is the sister who must take the step. Note the opening line:

> Hadrian: . . . it's *you* that I want, Matilda—not books, not poems!
> Matilda: What's stopping you, you fool?
> Hadrian: *(Goes to her awkwardly, like a boy. . . .)* Little girl with broken doll, Matilda! Matilda, Matilda, Matilda! Ring out little bells in heaven, little silver Matilda, little bells! *(He holds her against him, rocking and swaying in tender delight.)*
> Matilda: *(Laughs softly)* Don't—be crazy!
> Hadrian: Little silver Matilda, little bells, little bells! She's broken her doll. I broke it. She's slipped away and I've caught her—not far off. Little silver Matilda, little bells! *(Her head hangs so that her hair sweeps over her face. He tenderly brushes it back.)* Little Matilda, where are you hiding?
> Matilda: *(Softly and joyously.)* Nowhere! *(She throws her arms about him and returns his embrace with an equal abandon.)* Not any more!

The fantasy is complete. The brother can marry the sister and live happily ever after—free from guilt.

The sister will not appear as the sister again. But it should be noted that the girl Hadrian achieves is a child. He goes to her "awkwardly, like a boy" and she is the "little girl with broken doll" who has been hiding from him, but who now embraces him with "equal abandon." The girl child will remain the fantasy object or the remembered sexual ideal for a number of Williams' men. . . . [Clayton gives as examples: Dr. John's marriage to the girl child, Nellie, in *Summer and Smoke;* Kilroy's passion for the ever-virginal Esmeralda with her "childish nightgown" in *Camino Real;* Chance Wayne's despairing pursuit of his fifteen year old mistress, Heavenly, in *Sweet Bird of Youth;* and the ambiguous destructive relationship between the "cousins" Catharine and Sebastian in *Suddenly Last Summer.* One could add to the list the situation in *Baby Doll* and the brother-sister dependence of *The Two Character Play.*]

The progression of the sister figure in the works of Tennessee Williams is clear. A montage of his short stories and plays would present her as a child desired by the brother. She is a delicate and shy creature, and the brother figure experiences a great deal of guilt because of his desire for her. Though he may experience fantasies in which a relationship between them is realized in their youth, maturity brings estrangement. Eventually the sister is degraded and destroyed. Williams' characters will continue to show an attraction for the child-woman, and his mature women will continue to be portrayed as promiscuous and degraded or (in the case of the mother figure) dominant vampires who drain the man of vitality as they seek to subject him to their own will and purpose. The sister figure derives her importance from her family relationships. When divorced from the family, she becomes another familiar Williams' figure, The Delicate Lady. Deprived of the security offered by either family or marriage, she will turn to fantasy, promiscuity, and madness, as we see her in Blanche Du Bois in *A Streetcar Named Desire,* or Mrs. Harwicke-Moore in *The Lady of Larkspur Lotion,* or Edith Jelkes in *The Night of the Iguana,* or Miss Collins in *Portrait of a Madonna.* It is almost as though some ritual revenge were taking place as the woman who dares to leave childhood must be driven to the asylum or branded as a whore.

Tennessee Williams,
Theatre Poet in Prose

Frank Durham

Modern American attempts at verse drama have, on the whole, produced a harvest of respectable failures—*vide* the ambitious but incongruously rhetorical and ornate plays of Maxwell Anderson and the mannered and rather coldly calculated pieces by T. S. Eliot. Anderson bravely called for a return to poetry in the theatre and ground out a kind of blank verse that wore the label "Poetry"—in red paint;[1] while Eliot, likewise, wrote on the need for poetry in drama but staunchly maintained that the verse of the poet-dramatist should be so subtly disguised as, for the most part, not to sound like verse at all.[2] One of the difficulties regarding the use of verse in the modern theatre, as Eliot and MacLeish point out,[3] is the belief that the audience demands to see life as it is and that to such an audience poetry (or is it merely verse?) sounds "artificial." Eliot does say that there is a "peculiar range of sensibility [which] can be expressed by dramatic poetry, at its moments of greatest intensity," "a fringe of indefinite extent," beyond the capabilities of prose drama to express.[4] However, it is the contention of this paper that, while American drama has increasingly sought to portray this "peculiar range of sensibility," the most successful means of doing so has not been verse. It has, instead, been best portrayed by a new, or seemingly new, poetic drama which eschews verse for an eclectic but organic union of both verbal and non-verbal elements of the theatre, which many critics have recognized and which Tennessee Williams, one of its major practitioners, calls "plastic theatre." *The Glass Menagerie* will serve as a prime example of the form. . . .

What we have developed in twentieth-century America is a type

"Tennessee Williams, Theatre Poet in Prose" by Frank Durham. From the *South Atlantic Bulletin,* 36 (1971), 3–16. Copyright © 1971 *South Atlantic Bulletin.* Reprinted by permission of the publisher.

of poetic drama peculiarly relevant to our own time, a drama which maintains a speaking acquaintance with surface reality but which, through all the means at its disposal, probes into and bodies forth what Eliot calls that "peculiar range of sensibility," the inner truth, the often unutterable essences of human action and human emotion. As Alan Downer says:

> Thus the true poet of the theater is not necessarily concerned in the least with the traditional forms and language of poetry, but with making all the elements at his disposal—plot, actor, action, stage, lighting, setting, music, speech—unite to serve as a vehicle for his theme, his vision, or his interpretation of man's fate.[5] . . .

In his "Author's Production Notes" to *The Glass Menagerie,* in which he discusses at length such "extra-literary" elements as music and lighting, Williams makes clear that he is consciously striving to write this new type of poetic drama. Calling the piece "a memory play" and saying that it is therefore to be produced "with unusual freedom of convention," he says:

> Because of its considerably delicate or tenuous material, atmospheric touches and subtleties of direction play a particularly important part. Expressionism and all other unconventional techniques in drama have only one valid aim, and that is a closer approach to truth. When a play employs unconventional techniques, it is not, or certainly shouldn't be, trying to escape its responsibility of dealing with reality, or interpreting experience, but is actually or should be attempting to find a closer approach, a more penetrating and vivid expression of things as they are. The straight realistic play with its genuine frigidaire and authentic ice-cubes, its characters that speak exactly as its audience speaks, corresponds to the academic landscape and has the same virtue of photographic likeness. Everyone should know nowadays the unimportance of the photographic in art: that truth, life, or reality is an organic thing which the poetic imagination can represent or suggest, in essence, only through transformation, through changing into other forms than those which merely present an appearance.
>
> These remarks are not meant as a preface only to this particular play. They have to do with a conception of a new, plastic theatre which must take the place of the exhausted theatre of realistic conventions if the theatre is to resume vitality as a part of our culture.[6]

Thus Williams is consciously ushering in a new period in drama and a form, as Esther Merle Jackson says, distinctively and consciously American, a popular art form embodying all levels of American culture and life and in its intentions definitely poetic: "The search for a concrete expressive form—a shape congruent with poetic vision—is a motif that appears throughout the work of Williams."[7]

His realization of the need for "transformation" suggests Frost's idea: ". . . it is the height of poetry, the height of all thinking, the height of all poetic thinking, that attempts to say matter in terms of spirit and spirit in terms of matter." And, Frost continues, poetry (and thinking) is simply "saying one thing in terms of another."[8] Elsewhere Frost maintains that "every poem is a metaphor inside or it is nothing," and every poem is a symbol.[9] Certainly in *The Glass Menagerie,* often called a "lyric play," Williams is employing this concept of "transformation," of the dominant metaphor and symbol. Tom, his narrator-character, begins by telling us: "I give you truth in the pleasant guise of illusion." (p. 3)

In *The Glass Menagerie* there are two dominant metaphors or symbols. The more obvious is, of course, glass, as the title itself implies. Laura's glass animals, especially the unicorn, which is broken, symbolize the tenuousness of her hold on reality, the ease with which her illusion may be shattered. Of her, Williams says, ". . . the lovely fragility of glass which is her image." (p. vii) This symbol is relevant to the other characters also, for their ability to exist at all in the world rests on illusions as easily destroyed as the unicorn. Without her belief in her romantic past and in Laura's ultimate wooing by the non-existent Gentleman Caller, Amanda, who is the strongest, would be unable to face the harsh struggle for survival, would lose that fierce strength which in her is both comic and tragically admirable. At the touch of truth, her world will shatter into a thousand irretrievable fragments. The Gentleman Caller, Jim O'Connor, is also sustained by two illusions, that of his great success and promise in high school and that of his future triumph based on the empty slogans of his television night course: "Because I believe in the future of television! I want to be ready to go right up along with it. . . . I'm planning to get in on the ground floor. Oh, I've already made the right connections. All that remains now is for the industry itself to get under way—full steam! You know, *knowledge*—ZSZZppp! *Money*—ZZZZZZpp! POWER! Wham! That's the cycle democracy is built on!" (p. 54) Jim himself, as Tom tells us, is the momentary and disappointing embodiment of Laura and Amanda's illusion—"But having a poet's weakness for symbols, I am using this character as a symbol—as the long-delayed but always expected something we live for." (p. 3) Tom, despising his job in the warehouse, escaping temporarily into the fantasy world of the movies, cherishes the ideal of the absconded father ("He was a telephone man who fell in love with long distance. . . .") and envies Malvolio the Magician, who, nailed inside a coffin, "got out without removing one nail." (p. 19) But in Tom's case glass is both fragile and everlasting, for his physical escape brings no real liberation. Though he travels widely, the trap still holds him:

> Perhaps it was a familiar bit of music. Perhaps it was only a piece of transparent glass. . . . Perhaps I am walking along a street at night, in some strange city, before I have found companions, and I pass the lighted window of a shop where perfume is sold. The window is filled with pieces of colored glass, tiny transparent bottles in delicate colors, like bits of a shattered rainbow. Then all at once my sister touches my shoulder. I turn around and look into her eyes. (p. 62)

While glass is the more obvious of the metaphors or symbols which govern the play—and it is, to me, the symbol of the theme— the motion picture serves as the symbol determining the over-all form of the play. Tom, the narrator, through whose consciousness we see the entire action, tells us at the start, "The play is memory. . . . Being a memory play, it is dimly lighted, it is senti- mental, it is not realistic." (p. 3) Since it is Tom's memory and since Tom's escape from reality is the motion picture, Williams logically portrays Tom's memories in terms of the motion picture, the silent film even though dialogue is used. The structure and rhythmic flow of the scenes are like those of the motion picture. The screen device, generally omitted in production, resembles closely the use of subtitles on the silent screen, and Williams even employs simulated close-ups on several occasions, focusing his spotlight on indi- viduals or objects, such as the father's photograph, much in the manner of the camera.

Once Tom's initial address to the audience establishes the entire play as memory, the action begins. The opening scene, that of Amanda and Laura in the dining room at the rear of the living room, commences as if it were what in motion pictures is called a long shot, for the two women are seen through a pair of scrim curtains which achieve the effect of both unreality and distance. First, the scrim representing the outside wall is raised, and Tom joins the women. Then Williams calls for the raising of the inner scrim, and the whole effect is like that of a camera dollying in for a closer shot. In the most widely published version, though not in the acting edition, Williams calls for subtitles and images to be projected "on a section of wall between the front-room and the dining-room," like those of the silent film. In such films a subtitle was often used at the beginning of a scene to tell the audience what to expect, sometimes to give the mood or thematic significance of the images to follow. When Laura and Amanda are revealed the subtitle is "OU SONT LES NEIGES." Williams says that the screen device was originally intended

> to give accent to certain values in each scene. Each scene contains a particular point (or several) which is structurally most important. In an episodic play, such as this, the basic structure or narrative line may be obscured from the audience; the effect may seem fragmentary rather than architectural. . . . The legend or image upon the screen will strengthen the effect of what is merely allusion in the writing and allow the primary point to be made more simply and lightly than if the entire responsibility were on the spoken lines.[10]

In short, Williams is describing a structure remarkably close to that of the silent film—a series of short scenes, each making one or more points, with little or no transition between. The cumulative effect of these scenes, the relationships achieved by their juxtaposition and flow—these resemble what is in film called montage, originally associated with the work of Griffith and Eisenstein. Several critics have likened Williams' technique to that of the cinema and have used the term *montage* in their analyses of his structure.

In his comments on lighting and in his use of it in the play, Williams frequently suggests cinematic camera shots. He employs light, for example, for reaction close-ups. He says,

> Shafts of light are focused on selected areas or actors, sometimes in contradistinction to what is the apparent center. For instance, in the quarrel scene between Tom and Amanda, in which Laura has no active part, the clearest pool of light is on her figure. This is also true of the supper scene, when her silent figure on the sofa should remain the visual center. (p. vii)

In this way, the emphasis is not on the action itself but on a character's reaction to that action, the character highlighted as if in a close-up. And somewhat reminiscent of the diffused lighting Griffith used to employ to heighten the fragility of the young Lillian Gish or Mae Marsh, Williams calls for a special lighting of Laura: "The light upon Laura should be distinct from the others, having a peculiar pristine clarity such as the light used in early religious portraits of female saints or madonnas." (p. vii) He further says that throughout the production the light should suggest that in religious art, notably the work of El Greco, and that such lighting will make the use of the screen device more effective. The highlighting of the father's photograph has already been cited, and yet another outstanding example of the use of the cinematic close-up comes in Act I, Scene III, when Amanda tries to sell magazine subscriptions on the telephone. The light in the alley where Tom is fades out, *"and a head-spot falls on AMANDA, at phone in living-room."* (p. 13) The rest of the stage is dark, and Amanda stands alone in a circle of light revealing only her face. At the conclusion of her scene, *"Dining-room and living-room lights dim in. Reading lamp lights up at same time."* (p. 14) The close-up gives way to a longer shot of the whole room. Speaking generally of the lighting, Williams says: "A free, imaginative use of light can be of enormous value in giving a mobile, plastic quality to plays of a more or less static nature." (p. vii)

In the motion picture, both silent and sound, music has been a key element. For silent films whole scores were sometimes composed, for example, that played by the full orchestra which accompanied the initial road-showing of *The Big Parade* and *Ben Hur;* and for lesser films there was usually a music cue-sheet to guide the organist or pianist in his underlining of the mood or action of various scenes. Throughout the Acting Edition of *The Glass Menagerie* there are many music cues, and Williams stresses the importance of music as an "extra-literary accent" in the production. He calls for a "single recurring tune, 'The Glass Menagerie,' " to supply "emotional emphasis to suitable passages" (p. vi), and the mood of memory is established at the outset by *"dance-hall music . . . Old popular music of, say, 1915–1920 period."* (p. 1) The music, in general, is dim, like music far away. "It seems . . . to continue almost interminably and it weaves in and out of your preoccupied consciousness." It should be both gay and sad, expressing the beauty and the fragility of glass. "Both of these ideas should be woven into the recurring tune, which dips in and out of the play as if it were carried on wind that changes." It serves, too, as a link between the narrator and his story and helps to join the episodic, cinematic scenes: "Between each episode it returns as reference to the emotion, nostalgia, which is the condition of the play. It is primarily Laura's music and therefore comes out most clearly when the play focuses upon her and the lovely fragility of glass which is her image." (pp. vi-vii) Thus, as in the film, music is employed for both mood and transition, evoking the atmosphere of memory and establishing relationships between the individual scenes, stressing the fluidity of the progress of an otherwise static plot. It is significant that the first dramatic version of the story Williams did was a motion picture script for Metro-Goldwyn-Mayer.[11]

Other elements of the new non-verse poetic drama are also integral parts of the play. One of the most commented upon in the work of Williams is the symbol. In his preface to *Camino Real* Williams writes:

> I can't deny that I use a lot of those things called symbols, but being a self-defensive creature, I say that symbols are nothing but the natural speech of drama.
>
> We all have in our conscious and unconscious minds a great vocabulary of images, and I think all human communication is based on these images as are our dreams; and a symbol in a play has only one legitimate purpose, which is to say a thing more directly and simply and beautifully than it could be said in words.[12]

Sometimes, it is true, Williams tends to overwhelm us with symbols, apparently for their own sake, but in *The Glass Menagerie* the symbols are employed effectively as organic elements in his poetic concept. A simple listing of them would include such obvious ones as the Paradise Dance Hall, the fire escape, the father's photograph, "Blue Roses," the idea of the Gentleman Caller, and many others. But the one most often discussed is the glass unicorn from Laura's little menagerie. Williams' use of it reveals him at his poetic best, for the unicorn not only stands for something else (or for several something elses) but is used dramatically to symbolize a change in relationships between two of the characters. Generally, the glass menagerie, including the unicorn, portrays Laura, her fragility, her delicacy, her beauty, her unworldliness, and at the same time the unicorn in particular symbolizes her life-maintaining illusion, her idealized concept of Jim, the high school hero. When Jim appears in person, and the audience sees him as a sadly commonplace and frustrated human being, Laura still retains her illusions about him. But when she entrusts the unicorn in his hands, she says, "Oh, be careful—if you breathe, it breaks!" (p. 55) And Jim says, "Unicorns, aren't they extinct in the modern world?" (p. 55) Then in the ecstasy of the dance he knocks the unicorn from the table and it breaks— loses its horn, the thing that made it different from the others. And Laura, foreshadowing her coming disillusionment with the discovery of Jim's engagement, says, "The horn was removed to make him feel less—freakish! . . . Now he will feel more at home with the other horses, the ones who don't have horns. . . ." (p. 57) Thus Jim, the unicorn, the unique hero, subsides into the normal, the ordinary, himself destroying the aura of distinctiveness which Laura gave him, destroying her illusion—and yet she seems to accept this catastrophe with resignation. The unicorn has vanished, yes; but she still has her glass menagerie and the escape offered by her ancient phonograph records. One illusion is gone, but her other means of escape, her other illusions, still offer protection from life's harsh realities. Here the use of the symbol is not static but dynamic, embodying and underlining a major alteration in relationships.

While Eliot clung to the idea that poetic drama should be in verse, his concept of the effect which dramatic verse should create is relevant to Williams' use of language. Eliot says that audiences at a poetic, to him verse, drama

> expect poetry to be in rhythms which have lost touch with colloquial speech. What we have to do is to bring poetry into the world in which the audience lives and to which it returns when it leaves the theatre; not to transport the audience into some imaginary world totally unlike its own, an unreal world in which poetry is tolerated. What I should hope might be achieved, by a generation of dramatists having the benefit of our experience, is that the audience should find, at the moment of awareness that it is hearing poetry, that it is saying to itself: "*I* could talk poetry too!" Then we should not be transported into an artificial world; on the contrary, our own sordid, dreary daily world would be suddenly illuminated and transfigured.[13]

It is just this, I believe, that Williams is able to accomplish and to do so without resorting to the dangerous artificialities of verse. He takes colloquial speech, often the colloquial speech of the South, and through a keen ear for its rhythms and patterns, its imagery and symbolism, lifts it to the level of poetry. It is *real* speech, but real speech intensified and heightened so that it not only evokes the pleasure of recognition but communicates the inexpressible, the very essence of character, emotion, and situation in a way traditionally associated with poetry.

The Glass Menagerie is filled with such passages, expressing a broad spectrum of the emotions—Tom's hilariously pathetic parodies of motion pictures and stage shows, Amanda's tragi-comic magazine sales talk, and many others. The oft-cited jonquil speech is perhaps the best known. It has the patterned construction of a poem, its rhythms capture the emotions of its speaker, it embodies the comic-pathetic ideal of the gracious past, and it relies on floral imagery to enhance its resonance as poetry. Awaiting the arrival of the Gentleman Caller, Amanda dresses herself in the old gown of her youthful triumphs in the lost Never-Never Land of the Delta:

> This is the dress in which I led the cotillion. Won the cakewalk twice at Sunset Hill, wore one spring to the Governor's ball in Jackson!
> See how I sashayed around the ballroom, Laura?
> *[She raises her skirt and does a mincing step around the room.]*
> I wore it on Sundays for my gentlemen callers! I had it on the day I met your father—
> I had malaria fever all that spring. The change of climate from East Tennessee to the Delta—weakened resistance—I had a little temperature all the time—not enough to be serious—just enough to make me restless and giddy!—Invitations poured in—parties all over the Delta!—"Stay in bed," said Mother, "you have fever!"—but I just wouldn't.—I took quinine but kept on going, going!—Evenings, dances!—Afternoons, long, long rides! Picnics—lovely!—So lovely, that country in May.—All lacy with dogwood, literally flooded with jonquils!—That was the spring I had the craze for jonquils. Jonquils became an absolute obsession. Mother said, "Honey, there's no more room for jonquils." And still I kept on bringing in more jonquils. Whenever, wherever I saw them, I'd say, "Stop! Stop! I see jonquils!" I made the young men help me gather the jonquils! It was a joke, Amanda and her jonquils! Finally there were no more vases to hold them, every available space was filled with jonquils! No vases to hold them? All right, I'll hold them myself! And then I—*[She stops in front of the picture. MUSIC]* met your father!
> Malaria fever and jonquils and then—this—boy. . . .

Tom's final speech is another "set-piece," with its rhythmic flow, its recurrent imagery, its colloquial tone heightened by both the freight of the emotion and the suggestion of a pattern.

It is not only in the somewhat extended speeches that the poetic qualities are evident; many of the dialogues are made up of brief exchanges with the repetitive rhythmic patterns, almost like refrains, of verse but avoiding the rigidity of metre. Tom's teasing announcement of the visit of the Gentleman Caller is an example:

> *Tom:* We are going to have one.
> *Amanda:* What?
> *Tom:* A gentleman caller!
> *Amanda:* You mean you have asked some nice young man
>   to come over? . . .
> *Tom:* I've asked him to dinner.
> *Amanda:* You really did?
> *Tom:* I did.
> *Amanda:* And did he—accept?
> *Tom:* He did!
> *Amanda:* He did?
> *Tom:* He did.
> *Amanda:* Well, isn't that lovely!
> *Tom:* I thought you would be pleased.
> *Amanda:* It's definite, then?
> *Tom:* Oh, very definite.
> *Amanda:* How soon?
> *Tom:* Pretty soon.
> *Amanda:* How soon?
> *Tom:* Very, very soon. (pp. 27-28)

Here is approximately the give-and-take of traditional stichomythia retaining the quality of colloquialism.

Basic to the poetic qualities of Williams' language is his Southern origin, as several critics have noted. Marion Migid speaks of his

> long line, which achieves its most striking effects through a Steinian repetitiveness, through the use of unexpected archaisms, and the insertion of unexpected "literary" words and ironically elegant turns of phrase. It is a stylized rendering of Southern diction, which is more self-conscious, more evasive, but also more imaginative than Northern speech.[14]

Miss Jackson repeats this idea, stressing the fact that the natural symbolism of Southern diction has produced "a highly developed iconography." "This Southern aesthetic," she says, "has provided for the drama of Williams a kind of basic linguistic structure comparable to that which appeared in elementary stages of Greek tragedy."[15]

Modern studies of poetry have frequently developed the concept of the poet as a user of myth and a creator of new myths. Certainly in other plays, notably *Orpheus Descending, Suddenly Last Summer,* and *Camino Real,* underlying the action and characters are classical myths and pagan rituals. In his later plays especially, as Miss Jackson points out, Williams "has put together a kind of modern myth, a symbolic representation of the life of man in our time." She sees this myth as "synthetic," "composed, after the manner of cinematic montage, from the fragments of many ethical, philosophical, social, poetic, intellectual, and religious perspectives . . . the image of modern man caught between opposing logics—man in search of a means of reconciliation."[16] In *The Glass Menagerie* Williams reaches out tentatively for the materials of this myth. Basic to it is the idea of man's alienation from the world around him, man still clinging to old values in an environment where they are no longer relevant. Certain archetypal Williams figures begin to take shape in the play: the poet-wanderer, later to acquire sexual elements from D. H. Lawrence; the fragile girl threatened with destruction and either escaping into a dream world of the past or being corrupted by the jungle world of the present; the same girl in maturity, strong and defensive in her struggle against the present but finding sustenance through cherishing the ideal of lost grace and beauty. It is the myth of the alienated, the lost, seeking some sort of tenable posture in the present chaos. It is the source of the poet's vision. Williams himself says, "Personal lyricism is the outcry of prisoner to prisoner from the cell in solitary where each is confined for the duration of his life."[17]

One of the constants of lyric poetry, and of much other poetry as well, is its immediacy, its capturing of the moment, the intense moment of experience and insight. Man is in constant battle with Time the Destroyer, and poetry is one of his oldest means of achieving victory. In his use of time and in his attitude toward it, Williams is typically the poet. He says, "Snatching the eternal out of the desperately fleeting is the great magic of human existence."[18] In most of his plays his characters fight against time, its attrition and its ravages, and time becomes a major symbol of the adversary, malignant and malevolent. Amanda and Laura seek to turn time back, to recapture a past which they have perhaps idealized out of all semblance to reality but the very search for which gives meaning to their lives. On the other hand, Tom looks forward, toward a future time as an escape, but when that future becomes his present, he finds himself a prisoner of the past.

In *The Glass Menagerie* time is used another way, an equally poetic one. Tom stands with us in the immediate present. At the start he wears a merchant seaman's outfit indicative of escape from the physical past, of his having left his mother and sister behind. But through his consciousness we are carried back in time to his life in the drab apartment before his escape, and we retrace with him events leading to his decision to leave. Within this train of memory there are two types of time, the generalized and the specific, and through the use of these two we are given a deeper insight into the lives and relationships of the Wingfields. The first scene in the apartment, the dinner scene, is an example of generalized time. It is not any one particular dinner but a kind of abstraction of all the dinners shared by the trio in their life of entrapment. Amanda's admonitory speeches are ones often repeated, her stories of the seventeen gentlemen callers are oft-told tales—and Tom's irritated responses are those he makes each and every time the stories are retold. Amanda's telephone call to Ida Scott, with its pathetic attempts at salesmanship, is not one specific call, but, as the isolating spotlight tells us, it is an action out of time and place, the essence of a repeated action rather than a unique event. There are also unique moments in the parade of Tom's memory, highlights with a significance of their own—the imaginative reconstruction of the visit of Jim (for Tom was not present during some of the dialogue with Laura), for example. Through this multiple use of time Williams embodies both the concrete, the particular, and the general, the typical, his images often achieving the force of what Eliot has called the objective correlative of abstract truth.

From one point of view, as in *Death of a Salesman, The Glass Menagerie* actually transfixes and holds up for insight a single, brief moment of Tom's consciousness, a moment in the present in which, like Proust, he recapitulates the past, a past inextricably intertwined with the present and the future, freezes this moment— the intense moment of poetic insight, of lyric intuition. And this is often what a poem does. Williams is himself well aware of what he is doing. He says:

It is this continual rush of time, so violent that it appears to be screaming, that deprives our actual lives of so much dignity and meaning, and it is, perhaps more than anything else, the *arrest of time* which has taken place in a completed work of art that gives certain plays their feeling of depth and significance. . . . If the world of the play did not offer us this occasion to view its characters under that special condition of a *world without time,* then, indeed, the characters and occurrences of drama would become equally pointless, equally trivial, as corresponding meetings and happenings in life.

In such a timeless world, like that of Greek tragedy, man becomes aware of his potential nobility:

The audience can sit back in a comforting dusk to watch a world which is flooded with light and in which emotion and action have a dimension and dignity that they would likewise have in real existence, if only the shattering intrusion of time could be locked out.[19]

By arresting time, by embodying in a single moment the past, the present, and the future, by making this frozen moment one of tremendous intensity permitting an insight otherwise impossible, Williams has made *The Glass Menagerie* a lyric drama.

In conclusion, by utilizing many of the elements of poetry and the non-verbal facilities of the theatre—controlling metaphors and symbols, "transformation," lighting, music, movement, patterned colloquial speech, mythic elements, and the arresting of time to permit insight into the particular and the general—and by organically shaping these through a poet's vision—Williams in *The Glass Menagerie* exemplifies twentieth-century American poetic drama, free of the anachronism of verse, a poetic drama peculiarly adapted to the complexities of the present. Linking Williams with Arthur Miller, Kenneth Tynan says that both men, "committed to prose drama . . . have uncovered riches which make the English 'poetic revival' [of Eliot and Fry, for example] seem hollow, retrogressive, and—to use Cyril Connolly's coinage—praeterist."[20]

Notes

The author gratefully acknowledges the contributions to this essay by two of his graduate students, Jennifer Krugman and Mary Arnold Garvin.
[1]See his "A Prelude to Poetry in the Theatre," A Preface to *Winterset, Winterset* (New York: Anderson House, 1935). Also his "Poetry in the Theater," *Off Broadway: Essays about the Theater* (New York: William Sloane Associates, Inc., 1947).

[2]"Poetry and Drama," *On Poetry and Poets* (London: Faber and Faber, 1957), pp. 74–75.

[3]Eliot, *op. cit.,* p. 73, and Archibald MacLeish, "The Poet as Playwright," *Atlantic,* CXCV (Feb., 1955), 50.

[4]Eliot, *op. cit.,* pp. 86–87.

[5]*Fifty Years of American Drama, 1900–1950.* A Gateway Edition. (Chicago: Henry Regnery, 1966), p. 110.

[6]*The Glass Menagerie,* A Play in Two Acts. Acting Edition. (New York: Dramatists Play Service, 1948), p. vi. Hereafter quotations from this edition are followed in the text by page references in parentheses. With one exception, I have used this edition, which is supposed to be Williams' favorite, instead of the "bastardized script" published by New Directions in 1949 and widely anthologized. See L. A. Beaurline, "The Director, the Script, and Author's Revisions: A Critical Problem," in *Papers in Dramatic Theory and Criticism,* ed. David M. Knauf (Iowa City: University of Iowa Press, 1969), pp. 88–89.

[7]*The Broken World of Tennessee Williams* (Madison and Milwaukee: University of Wisconsin Press, 1965), pp. x-xii, 28.

[8]Robert Frost, "Education by Poetry," *Robert Frost: An Introduction,* ed. Robert A. Greenberg and James G. Hepburn (New York: Holt, Rinehart and Winston, Inc., 1961), p. 80. Reprinted from *Amherst Alumni Council News,* IV (March, 1931), 6–13.

[9]"The Constant Symbol," *Robert Frost: An Introduction,* p. 87. Reprinted from *Atlantic Monthly,* CLXXVIII (October, 1946), 50–52.

[10]"Production Notes," *The Glass Menagerie.* The New Classics. (New York: New Directions, 1949), p. x. This is the "bastardized script."

[11]Signi Lenea Falk, *Tennessee Williams.* Twayne's United States Authors Series No. 10. (New York: Twayne Publishers, Inc., 1961), p. 17. [But see Parker, "Texas Drafts," p. 53–61, for a more complex theory of the relation between the film script and play.]

[12]"Foreword," *Camino Real,* in *Six American Plays for Today,* selected by Bennett Cerf. Modern Library No. 38 (New York: Modern Library, 1961), p. 5. Originally in the *New York Times,* March 15, 1953.

[13]Eliot, "Poetry and Drama," p. 82.

[14]"The Innocence of Tennessee Williams," *Essays in the Modern Drama,* ed. Morris Freedman. (Boston: D. C. Heath & Co., 1964), pp. 282–283. Reprinted from *Commentary,* January, 1963.

[15]*The Broken World of Tennessee Williams,* p. 46.

[16]*Ibid.,* p. 54.

[17]"Person-To-Person," *Cat on a Hot Tin Roof.* Signet Book No. T 3547. (New York: The New American Library, n. d.), p. vii.

[18]"The Timeless World of a Play," *Perspectives on Drama,* ed. James L. Calderwood and Harold E. Toliver (New York: Oxford University Press, 1968), pp. 247–250. Reprinted from *The Rose Tattoo,* New Directions, 1950.

[19]*Ibid.,* pp. 248–249.

[20]"American Blues: The Plays of Arthur Miller and Tennessee Williams," *The Modern American Theater,* ed. Alvin B. Kernan (Englewood Cliffs, N. J.: Prentice-Hall, 1967), p. 36. Reprinted from *Curtains,* 1961.

The Glass Menagerie Revisited: Catastrophe Without Violence

Roger B. Stein

The Glass Menagerie (1945) was Tennessee Williams' first major theatrical success. Over the years he has written much, some of high quality indeed, but nothing better than this play which established him as an important post-war playwright. "The dramatist of frustration," John Gassner dubbed him in 1948 after *Streetcar,* but unlike most of his later plays, *The Glass Menagerie* projects not a series of violent confrontations leading to catastrophe but a vision of lonely human beings who fail to make contact, who are isolated from each other and from society, and who seem ultimately abandoned in the universe.

What holds the play together are Tom's remembrances of things past, not plot or characterization. Tom, the poet-narrator and author's surrogate, called "Shakespeare" in the warehouse, organizes the drama symbolically through language and image. This is the "new plastic theatre" of which Williams spoke in his production notes, a revelation not through dramatic struggle but through the allusive power of the word, the accretion of symbolic clusters which bear the meaning, reinforced dramaturgically through lighting, music, the distancing devices of a narrator and, as originally planned, of screen images.

The glass menagerie is itself the most obvious organizing symbol. It embodies the fragility of Laura's world, her search for beauty; it registers sensitively changes in lighting and stands in vivid contrast to the harshness of the outer world which can (and does) shatter it so easily. The unicorn can become the gift to Jim the

"*The Glass Menagerie* Revisited: Catastrophe Without Violence" by Roger B. Stein was abridged and revised by the author for Stephen Stanton, ed., *Tennessee Williams: A Collection of Critical Essays* (Englewood Cliffs, N.J.: Prentice-Hall, 1971). It was originally published in the *Western Humanities Review,* 18 (Spring, 1964), 141–153. Copyright © 1964 by *Western Humanities Review.* Reprinted by permission of the author and the publisher.

Gentleman Caller, whose anticipation and appearance form the plot of the play, only when it has lost its mythical uniqueness, the horn, when dream becomes momentarily possibility before it is obliterated at the end. The magic of Prince Charming's kiss can not work ("Stumblejohn," he brands himself in the published version of the play, taking on for the moment Laura's crippled condition). The "little silver slipper of a moon" on which Amanda has asked Laura to wish becomes an ironic image of Laura's isolated condition, but Amanda, wrapped up in her own illusions and selling magazine subscriptions and brassieres (like the "Gay Deceivers" with which she tries to stuff Laura before Jim appears) prefers to believe not in Tom's favorite D. H. Lawrence, but in Cinderella and courtly love and *Gone With the Wind,* the novel to which she compares Bessie May Harper's latest effort in *The Homemaker's Companion.* The ironies of the allusive imagery proliferate: Amanda's heroic efforts as homemaker are unsuccessful (the father appears only as a happy doughboy photographic image), and Margaret Mitchell's depression romance about the desirable Scarlett O'Hara in a lost Eden, a South fantasized in the national imagination during the Depression, only makes Laura look more forlorn. Finally one may note that the title image itself of *Gone With the Wind* underlines the evanescent quality of this dream and all of the Wingfields' illusions. As such, it points directly to the last line of the play and Tom's injunction to "Blow out your candles, Laura."

On the level of plot, this widening circle of reference enhances the credibility of the dramatic situation. Given Amanda's sham version of idealized love and a fantasy past, how could the Gentleman Caller's visit be other than a failure? Despite Amanda's dress which is "historical almost," despite the attempt to live in the nineteenth century when the electric power goes off, Jim is not Rhett Butler but an "emissary from a world of reality," as Tom calls him, an engaged twentieth-century man on vacation. The flickering candlelight of Jim's scene with Laura is not enough to sustain the illusion; at the end of their scene this illusion collapses and we are left in darkness.

But *The Glass Menagerie* is built upon more than the poignant plot of illusion and frustration in the lives of little people. Williams has deepened the losses of individuals by pointing to social and even spiritual catastrophe. The time of the play is 1939, as the narrative frame makes explicit both at the beginning and the end. The life of illusion is not confined to the Wingfields alone. As Tom says, "the huge middle class of America was matriculating in a school for the blind." What he calls the "social background" of the play has an important role. The international backdrop is Guernica and the song America sings is "The World is Waiting for the Sunrise," for the sober truth is that America is still in the depression and on the brink of war. The note of social disaster runs throughout the drama, fixing the lives of individuals against the larger canvas.

Amanda's anxieties are in large part economic and there is money behind many of her illusions: her mythical suitors were all wealthy men, as are her magazine heroes; she computes the money Tom would save by giving up smoking. When Tom complains of the grimness of life in the shoe factory, she replies, "Try and you will SUCCEED!" If this is another of Amanda's illusions, it is one shared by her fellow Americans, for "try and you will succeed" is the traditional motto of the American dream of success, the theme of confident self-reliance canonized in the romances of Horatio Alger.

It is not Amanda, however, but Jim, the emissary from reality, who is the chief spokesman for the American dream. To Jim the warehouse is not a prison but a rung on the ladder toward success. He believes in self-improvement through education, and the lecture on self-confidence which he reads to Laura is part of the equipment of the future executive. He is awed by the fortune made in chewing gum and rhapsodizes on the theme of the future material progress of America: "All that remains is for the industry to get itself under way! Full steam—*Knowledge—Zzzzzp! Money—Zzzzzp! Power!* That's the cycle democracy is built on!"

Yet when the theme of success is superimposed upon the lives of the characters, the social irony emerges. Father was not the successful businessman, but a telephone man who "fell in love with long distances." Tom, the substitute father, refuses to pay the light bill, plunges his family into darkness, and then runs out, and Amanda sells subscriptions and brassieres only at the loss of her dignity. Jim's own dream of success seems to have reached its peak in high school. (Williams later explored this theme more fully in *Cat on a Hot Tin Roof*.) The trek upward through the depression years is disappointing, but the indomitable optimist is not discouraged.

The experience of the 1930s did not turn Williams into a proletarian writer or social realist, but it did open up for him a darker vision of American life which he suggests to his audience but which is denied to his characters, still "matriculating in a school for the blind": a belief that the American dream is itself a sham and a failure. In his essay "The Catastrophe of Success," Williams said that "the Cinderella story is our favorite national myth, the corner-stone of the film industry if not of the Democracy itself." The social catastrophe inherent in *The Glass Menagerie* lies precisely in the fact that Laura is *not* Cinderella: the silver slipper does not finally fit, and Jim is not Prince Charming but one of the innumerable Americans who would soon be moving overseas in troop ships. As Tom says at the end, "for nowadays the world is lit by lightning! Blow out your candles, Laura—and so goodbye. . . ." The world which had been waiting for the sunrise burst with bombardments instead, and the lives of the Wingfields at the end are absorbed in the larger social tragedy.

Williams goes even further than this, however. The end of the play involves more than just the snuffing out of Laura's hope; it is even more than social tragedy. It is a *Götterdämmerung.* For the candles and the lightning which close the play have appeared together before. We are told by Amanda that the candelabrum "used to be on the altar at the church of the Heavenly Rest. It was melted a little out of shape when the church burnt down. Lightning struck it one spring." Amanda's comment opens up another dimension of the drama, and reminds us that Williams, inheritor of a Southern religious tradition which includes writers like Faulkner and Robert Penn Warren, has persistently drawn upon the language of Christian symbolism to define his characters' human situations. Amanda's quiet comment is a far cry from the hysterical ravings of the defrocked Reverend T. Lawrence Shannon in *Night of the Iguana* about wanting "to go back to the church and preach the gospel of God as Lightning and Thunder." The pervasive religious overtones of *The Glass Menagerie* never obscure the literal line of the story or seem self-conscious, as they frequently do in the later plays. Ultimately they try to locate the catastrophe at the end beyond human pathos and social tragedy.

Williams' stage directions clearly indicate his intention. The lighting for Laura should resemble that "used in early religious portraits of female saints or madonnas." The scene where Tom tells his mother that a Gentleman Caller will appear Williams entitles "Annunciation." The dressing of Laura for the Caller's appearance should be "devout and ritualistic." During her scene with Jim she is lit "inwardly with altar candles," and when Jim withdraws after kissing her Williams informs us that the "holy candles in the altar of Laura's face have been snuffed out. There is a look of almost infinite desolation."

Those overtones extend beyond Williams' hints to the director and become part of the fabric of dramatic action. The first scene in both the acting version and the library edition of the play opens on this note. In the former, Amanda narrates her "funny experience" of being denied a seat in the Episcopal church because she has not rented a pew. The idea of the Wingfields' exclusion from Christian ceremony is established thus at the outset, and it is underlined by the ensuing talk of digesting food, mastication, and salivary glands. In the Wingfield apartment, eating is an animal process only; it lacks ritual significance. The library edition opens with Amanda's call to Tom, "We can't say grace until you come to the table," and then moves on to the question of digestion. The lines are different, but their import is the same. When the Gentleman Caller comes, the scene is repeated, only this time it is Laura whose absence holds up "grace."

Amanda, who condemns instinct and urges Tom to think in terms of the mind and spirit, as "Christian adults" do, is often characterized in Christian terms. Her music, in the library edition, is "Ave Maria." As a girl she could only cook angel food cake. She urges Laura, "Possess your soul in patience," and then speaks of her dress for the dinner scene as "resurrected" from a trunk. Her constant refrain to Tom is "Rise an' Shine," and she sells subscriptions to her friends by waking them early in the morning and then sympathizing with them as "Christian martyrs." Laura is afraid to tell her mother she has left the business school because "when you're disappointed, you get that awful suffering look on your face, like the picture of Jesus' mother in the museum!"

The next picture Laura mentions is the one of Jim in the yearbook. Though the context seems secular enough at this point—Jim is a high school hero—his religious function emerges later on. In the "Annunciation" scene, when Amanda learns that the Gentleman Caller's name is O'Connor, she says, "that, of course, means fish—tomorrow is Friday!" The remark functions not only literally, since Jim is Irish Catholic, but also figuratively, for the fish is the traditional symbol of Christ. In a very real sense both Amanda and Laura are searching for a Savior who will come to help them, to save them, to give their drab lives meaning.

Tom is unable to play this role himself. Though he appears as the angel of the Annunciation, he denies the world of belief and in a bitter speech to his mother calls himself "El Diablo." With him Christian terms appear only as imprecations: "what in Christ's

name" or "that God damn Rise and Shine." When Tom returns
home drunk one night, he tells Laura of a stage show he has seen
which is shot through with Christian symbolism, none of which he
perceives. Here the magician, Malvolio, whose name suggests bad
will, dislike, or even hate, plays the role of the modern Christ. He
performs the miracle of turning water into wine and then goes on to
blasphemy by turning the wine into beer and then whiskey. He also
produces his proper symbol, the fish, but it is gold-fish, as if stained
by modern materialism. Most important, he escapes from a nailed
coffin. But Tom reads the symbolism of this trick in personal terms
only. When Laura tries to keep him from awakening Amanda, Tom
retorts:

> Goody, goody! Pay 'er back for all those "Rise an' Shines." You know
> it don't take much intelligence to get yourself into a nailed-up coffin,
> Laura. But who in hell ever got himself out of one without removing
> one nail?   (Scene 4)

The illumination of the father's photograph at this point suggests
one answer to this question, but the pattern of Christian imagery in
the drama, especially when reinforced here by the "Rise an' Shine"
refrain, should suggest to us another answer—the resurrection
itself—which Tom's rejection of Christian belief prevents him from
seeing.

It remains therefore for Jim to come as the Savior to this Friday
night supper. The air of expectancy is great, with the ritualistic
dressing of Laura, the tension, and the oppressive heat. Jim's arrival
is marked by the coming of rain, but the hopes of fertility and
renewal which this might suggest are soon dashed. Laura's attempt
to come to the dinner table is a failure, signaled by a clap of thunder,
and Tom's muttered grace, "For these and all thy mercies, God's
Holy Name be praised," is bitterly ironic, mocked by what follows.
The only paradise within reach is Paradise Dance Hall, with its
"Waste Land" mood of slow and sensuous rhythms and couples
kissing behind ashpits and telephone poles, "the compensation for
lives that passed . . . without any change or adventure," as Tom
remarks. The failure of electric power after dinner—previsioning
the blackout of the world—leads to Amanda's joking question,
"Where was Moses when the lights went off?" This suggests another
savior who would lead his people from the desert into the promised
land, but the answer to her question is "In the dark."

Jim's attempt to play the modern savior is an abysmal failure. In the after-dinner scene, he offers Laura the sacrament—wine and "life-savers," in this case—and a Dale Carnegie version of the Sermon on the Mount—self-help rather than divine help—but to no avail. At the end of the play Laura and Amanda are, as the joke bitterly reminds us, "in the dark," and Tom's last lines announce the final failure, the infinite desolation: "For nowadays the world is lit by lightning. Blow out your candles, Laura—and so good-bye. . . ."

Here as elsewhere in his plays Williams draws upon his frightened characters' preference for soft candlelight to harsh daylight or electric bulbs, not only because it serves him dramaturgically to establish his conception of a new plastic theater where evanescent characters and images flicker across the stage momentarily, but also because his characters so often want to withdraw from the blinding light of reality into the softer world of illusion. At the end of *The Glass Menagerie,* however, the blackout is even more catastrophic, for it not only envelops the Laura of Tom's memory and serves as another reminder of the blackout of war which shrouds the world: it is also the denial of any final "Rise an' Shine" for these frail creatures. The church has been struck by lightning, and all hope of resurrection has been lost in this damned universe where belief turns into metaphor, where humankind seems abandoned by its God, and where the echoes of prayer are heard only in blasphemy or irony. The bleakness of Williams' vision in *The Glass Menagerie* is complete. If Tom is released finally, it is in the words of Job, "And I only am escaped alone to tell thee." It is as the author's surrogate, as writer and chronicler of catastrophe, that he emerges at the end.

Postscript 1976

Published criticism of *The Glass Menagerie* since this essay was originally written in 1964 has confirmed in other particulars my sense of the importance of the religious language of the drama, and my interpretation, in turn, has been used to attack Marxist readings of the play as a dramatization of the disintegration of a lower middle class family under a ruthless capitalist system during the Depression.[1] It is a tribute to the play's richness that it has stimulated both kinds of criticism. What I would emphasize now in rethinking these issues is that a Marxist analysis of the play, though incomplete, is both ideologically accurate and descriptively useful. Williams did serve his aesthetic apprenticeship during the 1930s, and in the first part of his opening description of the apartment building he does point us towards a class analysis of "this largest and fundamentally enslaved section of American society." But this intention loses force in the last few words of the paragraph.

Williams' understanding of and compassion for the illusions of the Wingfields are based upon an implicit recognition that work in America is alienating drudgery: Rubicam's Business College for Laura, selling illusions for Amanda, Continental Shoes for Tom ("the warehouse is where I work, not where I know people," he tells Amanda, with, as it turns out, devastating consequences for Laura). They are indeed victims of a larger social failure, for humane democratic values have been redefined and inverted by Jim, the economic system's apologist, as a use of knowledge to gain power and money. In this Depression world, as Tom tells us, it takes a war to make adventure available to the masses, to release them from the social trap. Which is of course precisely what happened.

In the light of these social clarifications, it seems to me now that Williams' religious language in the play becomes—however unconsciously—a strategic mode for evading the implications of his social analysis, about which, like Amanda ("We live in such a mysterious universe, don't we?"), he is finally muddled. If his sense of cosmic catastrophe and of the metaphysical abandonment of his characters in the universe is, as I have shown, in some ways a great dramatic and linguistic strength of the play, it is from another point of view a typical weakness of Williams and American writers in general. Failing in their art to explore humankind adequately in society, they shift responsibility for the human condition to the divine and write metaphysical romances rather than trenchant social drama, in a series of dramatic gestures which fluctuate between Byronic defiance and ultimate despair. This weakness is especially apparent in Williams' later plays, which frequently exploit what I would call the romance of violence. The greatness of *The Glass Menagerie,* as art and as human statement, still lies in Williams' ability at that point in his career to sustain a sense of the individual, the social, and the religious dimensions of our experience poised in delicate poetic balance.

Notes

[1]Gilbert Debusscher, in "Tennessee Williams' Unicorn Broken Again," *Revue belge de Philologie et d'Histoire,* 49 (1971), 875–85, builds upon my analysis and weakens the argument of Grigor Pavlov's Marxist "Comparative Study of Tennessee Williams' *The Glass Menagerie* and *Portrait of a Girl in Glass,*" *Annuaire de l'Université de Sofia,* Faculté des Lettres, 62 (1968), 111–31.

[For another Marxist reading of Williams, see Maya M. Koreneva, *Contemporary American Drama:* 1945–70, published doctoral dissertation (Moscow: Gorky Institute of World Literature, Academy of Sciences, U.S.S.R., 1975). She thinks that Williams' significance lies in his exposure (in the early plays) of decadent social conditions in America at the time of World War II. When he switched from social to sexual studies, however, he ceased to be a playwright of the first rank.—*Stephen Stanton.*]

Two Memory Plays:
The Glass Menagerie and
After the Fall

Paul T. Nolan

For the past seventy-five years or more, playwrights have attempted to move beyond the traditional scope of the drama—*to show* an action—to deal directly with the source of action itself, the mind. The soliloquy of drama, once an embellishment, an aside, has become the basis of the entire play in such forms as the "dream play" and "expressionistic drama." An interesting and important achievement in this search to stage directly the mind of man is the "memory play," a term that has been in use by dramatic critics for only about twenty years. It is now commonplace to describe such plays as *The Glass Menagerie*[1] and *After the Fall*[2] by the term "memory plays"; but no critic, to my knowledge, has yet suggested that this is a separate form, built upon a different set of assumptions from the traditional drama-of-action and different, too, from such mind-searching plays as Strindberg's *Dream Play* or Kaufman and Connelly's *Beggar on Horseback*. The new "memory play," unlike the dream play and expressionistic drama, is a projection of the conscious mind; and, unlike the traditional drama-of-action, it is concerned only with that action that is understood and retained in the mind of the protagonist.

The memory of a character has, of course, always been a part of drama. It is the memory of the Chorus that informs the audience of the events leading to the final catastrophe of Aeschylus' *Agamemnon*. A single actor's memory, moreover, has long been a part of drama. Hamlet's soliloquies are essentially his statements of his memory of the past. The memory of Willy Loman in *Death of a Salesman* is

Excerpted from "Two Memory Plays: *The Glass Menagerie* and *After the Fall*" by Paul T. Nolan. From *The McNeese Review*, 17 (1966), 27–38. Copyright © 1966 by Paul T. Nolan. Reprinted by permission of the author.

projected into a character that may be seen by the audience; Uncle Ben, as he is seen in the play, is Willy's memory of him—not a character created from the person himself.

There is, however, a difference between "memories in drama," either recalled or projected, and a "memory play." In plays that merely use memory as part of the drama, the world of the drama is rooted in some kind of a real world beyond the characters themselves, a world shown or suggested, against which the audience must evaluate the truth or falsity, accuracy or distortion of every act, speech, and memory.

In the memory play as a particular form, the world of the drama *is* the memory of a single character, the narrator-protagonist. Tom Wingfield in *The Glass Menagerie* and Quentin in *After the Fall* show the audience their memories, and that memory is all the world there is. The memory play is set in the conscious mind of the protagonist, and it stands aloof from outside testimony. If the play is true, the memory is true.

Tom Wingfield assumes the "truth" of his memory, but he recognizes that the world of his memory is full of distortions. He promises, in his opening speech, "truth in the pleasant guise of illusion," but as he continues his opening narration, it becomes obvious that he is speaking of the relationship of the play to his memory, not of his memory to any fact beyond the theatre. The play, he suggests, has a "social background," depression America; but beyond the fact that Tom's memory was formed in turbulent times, the background is meaningless to the play.

"The play is memory," Tom tells his audience. "Being a memory play, it is dimly lighted, it is sentimental, it is not realistic." One of the characters in the play, he suggests, came into his memory and remained there without distortion, "the gentleman caller who appears in the final scenes." "He is," says Tom, "the most realistic character in the play, being an emissary from a world of reality that we were somehow set apart from." The other characters in the play—the narrator, himself; Amanda, his mother; Laura, his sister; and "the larger-than-life-size photograph" of "our father"— clearly are characters of the memory. Even the character of the gentleman caller, Tom qualifies, is not wholly realistic; "But since I have a poet's weaknesses for symbols, I am using this character also as a symbol; he is the long awaited but always expected something that we live for."

In the list of "Characters" Williams gives his "objective evaluations" of the characters: "Amanda . . . much to admire in Amanda, and as much to love and pity as there is to laugh at . . . Laura . . . too exquisitely fragile to move from the shelf. Tom . . . not remorseless, but to escape from a trap he has to act without pity. Jim . . . a nice, ordinary, young man." It would be a mistake, however, to confuse these evaluations with the characters of the memory. "Laura's situation," for example, is described in the list of "Characters" as being "even graver" than Amanda's; but in the world of Tom's memory, she is stronger, not merely than Amanda but than Tom, too. Tom might have said, "Oh, Laura, Laura, I tried to leave you behind, but [you are stronger, *rather than*] I am more faithful than I intended to be!" And Tom, himself, does not escape "his trap," no matter what the "Character" notes say. This is not to suggest that Williams' character notes may not be helpful to the actors playing the roles; it is, however, to argue that finally we must accept the characters as they appear in Tom's memory or not at all. Amanda, whatever a person like such a character may be in life, is a monster in Tom's memory, and the monster is all the Amanda there is in *The Glass Menagerie*.

Any audience has the right, of course, to ask what are the relationships between the world of the play and the world outside the play that is being mirrored. When that world is one that we can see about us in time or in space, we can, by our own standards, evaluate the truthfulness of the play-world by comparing it with our concept of the world-outside that it reflects. But in a memory play, the world outside the play is the memory of the narrator and our only access to that world is through the memory of the narrator-protagonist in the play. As a social comment, we may, of course, complain that the memory of the narrator is a distortion of an outside world that it remembers; but this is simply to observe that a subjective memory of a person and an event is not an objective recording, a fact of dramatic composition that the playwright, by using the form of the memory play, has insisted upon from the first.

The narrator in the memory play promises his audience only that he will show the people, the events, the cause-effect relationships that make up his memory. In *After the Fall*, it is suggested that in the process the audience will be shown how the character of the narrator-protagonist came to accept his memory and live with it; and in *The Glass Menagerie*, it is suggested that in the process the audience will be shown why the narrator-protagonist is taking leave of his memory—"Blow out your candles, Laura. . . ." But in both plays, once the audience has accepted the world of the memory, all objective criticism in terms of economic theory, psychological realism, or philosophical logic becomes impossible, or at least fruitless.

The advantage to the playwright of the memory play is quite clearly that he can unroll his memory—the real history of his character—without having it edited, corrected, challenged. The reviewer for *The Village Voice,* who insisted that there is a one-for-one relationship between Quentin and Arthur Miller, saw *After the Fall* as a public confession of the playwright: "Quentin, at all times, remains Arthur Miller, questing among his moral flash-cards, muscling his way toward the perfect analysis. . . ."[3] Undoubtedly, the writer of the "memory play" will create a narrator-protagonist whose history closely suggests his own. Miller and Quentin both married three times; both had, for a second wife, a public performer who took her own life. Williams and Tom Wingfield both had fathers who, in one way or another, "deserted"; both had Southern-belle mothers and "psychologically crippled" sisters. To acknowledge these similarities, however, is to do no more than to say that a playwright must mirror the world that he sees; and the author of a memory play must work in terms of his own memory. He can see no other. . . .

But it is an error to think that a memory play will succeed because of the private memories of the playwright. The memory play pleases for the same reason any other play pleases; it offers its audience an involvement in a world that seems more real (or more attractive) than its own. The audience must judge whether or not to be concerned with the characters and their problems; but, unlike the audience of a play that pictures an objective world, the audience of a memory play is really unable to measure the subject against the portrait.

The narrator-protagonist in a memory play tells the audience that he is the result of his memory. He offers to show this memory in the form in which it exists at the moment of the play. Arthur Ganz complains that *After the Fall* is "not a memory play—but a Chronicle History" and argues that after the first quarter of the play the memory technique is abandoned as a meaningful structure.[4] It would be fairer to suggest that Quentin's memory deals with episodes first thematically, then chronologically. *The Glass Menagerie,* it should be noted, follows a chronological order through-that," the "economy is not like that," and "things do not happen that way," if the whole form of the play proclaims, "Perhaps not, but this is the way in which my memory has stored them."

One whose primary concern is with ideas can, however, take comfort that there is no need for such judgments of a memory play. In such a play, the narrator-protagonist will tell his audience that he is in the midst of a problem, a problem created by a memory that is hard to bear. He will then unroll that memory, *not* selecting those details that would most meaningfully dramatize his problem but *rather* dramatizing those details which have been selected for storage in the memory. Since it is suggested that it is the memory that is the man, it is, of course, further suggested that an open examination of the whole memory will lead to an understanding of that man, perhaps implying that when the man comes to an understanding of himself (his memory), he will be able to act. It is probably further suggested that as the memory becomes more detailed, better ordered, and more objective, the narrator-protagonist is moving toward understanding.

The characters in the memory play exist only in relationship to the narrator-protagonist. They may appear to him to be weak or strong, heroes or villains; but the point of their interest is not what they *are* but what they are *to the narrator*. Amanda for Tom is so monstrous a character that he is made ill by her mere mundane comments. It is really not important, although we may note it in passing, that she was for the playwright a woman of some courage.

In retrospect, of course, the critic may ask what relationship there is between the *memory* and the *reality* that gave it its nature; but the focus in the memory play, it seems to me, should be on the narrator-protagonist, the owner of the memory, how he came into possession of it, in what form it possesses him, and, finally, what will result from it.

When the curtain rises on *The Glass Menagerie,* the audience meets Tom Wingfield, the narrator-protagonist, "dressed as a merchant sailor," entering "from an alley," performing an amateur trick of magic. He comes as a self-proclaimed philosopher: "I give you truth. . . ." The *truth,* somehow, is associated with the past decade—the age of depression, "when the huge middle class of America was matriculating in a school for the blind." But the immediate truth has to do with Tom and his associations with out. Admittedly, there is something frustrating about a critical examination of a memory play, especially for a critic whose first concern is with "ideas." One cannot carp that "people are not like "other characters . . . my mother . . . my sister . . . and a gentleman caller. . . . There is a fifth character . . . our father." The elder Wingfield has deserted his family, for what exact cause we never learn; but in Tom's memory, "He was a telephone man who fell in love with long distance; he gave up his job with the telephone company and skipped the light fantastic out of town. . . . The last we heard from him was a picture post-card . . . containing a message of two words—'Hello—Goodbye!' and no address." For Tom, this cryptic message is all the memory there is, and Tom's final words in the play, ". . . and so good-bye . . .," are a conscious echo of the father. After a long reflection, one may wonder if Tom in following his "father's footsteps," attempting to find in "motion what was lost in space," ever had doubts concerning his father's wisdom. Such a concern, however, is beyond the scope of the play. Tom's memory, the play itself, does not move forward from the opening speech. The play is dramatic in that the memory is revealed like an action, but the memory *itself* is static. The character of Tom is not affected by the revelation.

As a memory play, *The Glass Menagerie* is not essentially about other people, but rather about Tom's memory of other people. Even in the most tense conflicts between Amanda and Laura, the audience is aware of Tom's standing in the wings waiting; and after a scene is over, he will by a comment or gesture—"TOM motions to the fiddles in the wings"—remind the audience that it is unimportant as to what effect the scene has for them. It is only important what effect it had on him.

In the simplest terms, *The Glass Menagerie* sets forth Tom's "reasons" for his renunciation of the conventional goals of the society in which he lives. The play is his memory, and his memory—not a rational analysis of it—is his evidence. It is not necessary to accept the memory as a valid artifact of the deed. It is necessary that one accept the memory itself as a fact, the one fact of Tom's existence. Tom's world—from a distance "lit by lightning," the war in Europe—is his description, not his defense. The world beyond, in rags and at war, is beyond his responsibility, beyond his memory.

The Glass Menagerie has a purity of genre that does not exist in *After the Fall*. Miller's first directions inform that "The action takes place in the mind, thought, and memory" of Quentin; and the addition of "mind" and "thought" marks the difference in the plays themselves.

After the Fall takes place in the mind of Quentin, but unlike Tom, Quentin does not accept his memory as the only truth that exists for him. Tom offers the memory of a single, trivial episode (set in a terrible, shadowy world which he acknowledges only faintly) as truth. Quentin brings a broader memory—one that encompasses the lives of others, one that tries to reconcile the "blasted stone tower of a German concentration camp" with personal fears that he is sacrificing his career, perhaps "trying to destroy myself"—as *one* piece of evidence which he intends to examine with his mind and reason (thought). Tom is a poet who finds truth in a symbol; Quentin is a lawyer who finds meaning in the law. Both characters escape from intolerable situations; but Tom is eager to escape, certain that he can trust the symbols of his memory. Quentin can leave only with the most profound regrets and feelings of guilt for his lack of regret. Tom feels no responsibility even for the immediate world in which he lives; Quentin feels a responsibility even for the world beyond his control, beyond his understanding. He feels responsibility for the Nazi terror: "Who can be innocent again on this mountain of skulls?" He feels responsibility for all the deaths he knows, a personal responsibility: ". . . I loved them all, all! And gave them willingly to failure and to death that I might live. . . ."

Tom has control of his memory. *The Glass Menagerie* has the simple cause-effect action of the well-made play. As anything else but a memory play, it would be a pathetic little sentimental piece, not even as large as Thornton Wilder's *Happy Journey to Camden and Trenton*. *The Glass Menagerie,* in fact, suggests a larger world by the mere fact that Tom, *willfully,* discards from this memory everything beyond his physical senses. He can see the lightning of World War II, but he cannot see the world that is lit by it. Tom has complete faith in his memory, but this memory is as rigorously controlled in its selection of details as is Amanda's memory of her youth; and he is as devoted to the movies, the casual companion, and the symbol out of context as Amanda is to the D.A.R., the genteel social amenities, and the wonderful new serial by Bessie Mae Harper.

Quentin has no such control of his memory. The play sprawls like a novel by Tolstoy. Allan Lewis argues that in *After the Fall,* Miller's real problem is "original sin," from the fall of man to the horror of post-war Europe; his real audience is not, as Tom Wingfield's is, his slightly inferior contemporaries, but rather the maker of all truth. The opening lines, "Hello! God, it's good to see you again!", according to Lewis, should be punctuated, "Hello, God. It's good to see you again."[5] Quentin brings his memories and his beliefs to the listener, and in a series of agonizing sessions, he asks to have these memories fitted to his beliefs or to have his beliefs altered to fit his memories. Standing between the belief and the memory is the questioning mind, doubting itself, to be sure, weary with failure, but never really abdicating—not to the memory, not to the old beliefs, not to a new philosophy of despair.

Both *The Glass Menagerie* and *After the Fall* have autobiographical elements in them. Maggie is a memory of Marilyn Monroe, perhaps Arthur Miller's memory, perhaps only the audience's hopes or fears that this is a personal memory since it seems to agree with its own. Laura is a memory of Tennessee Williams' sister. Critics have, however, complained only about Miller's use of such personal history and, at that, only such personal history as relates to Marilyn Monroe (Maggie), although, in truth, Maggie is a good deal more attractive character than are Mother, Father, or Louise—all of whom are, seemingly also characterizations of people close to Miller. The reason for this complaint is, I think, not merely the general feeling of guilt that many Americans have about the death of Marilyn Monroe, but it is that *After the Fall* is a memory play that is a part of our world. *The Glass Menagerie,* on the other hand, is a memory play of a world that is "somehow set apart."

The World of *After the Fall* is full of people striving, no matter how foolishly, for goals that are important. It is a world, moreover, of size and power. There is no value judgment intended in this observation, but it is obvious that while Tom Wingfield is a boy running away from his small world, Quentin is a man trying to make complex choices, trying to live in a very large world. Beyond a few flippant comments, there is no world in *The Glass Menagerie* beyond the physical reach of Tom Wingfield. Quentin's world, by contrast, is so large that even with "memory, mind and thought," Quentin's problem is essentially finding some means of coming to workable terms with that world. . . .

The characters within this wider world have more active, more classically dramatic, lives than the characters of *The Glass Menagerie,* who could summarize their lives briefly: tried one small thing once, feebly; failed, and resigned. But a dozen of the characters in *After the Fall* and perhaps two who do not appear on stage—Maggie's Judge Cruse and Mother's Dr. Strauss—have biographies in the play, complete enough to make them the central characters in drama of their own.

The play is Quentin's "spiritual autobiography" to be sure; but within his autobiography are the complete lives of Rose, his mother; his father; Dan, his brother; Quentin's "women"—Louise, Maggie, Holga, Felice, Elsie, Lou, Mickey, and the Rev. Harley Barnes. Miller uses characters both to show Quentin's problems and to suggest the multiplicity of personal dramas taking place within the central action. Such a use is not a violation of the memory-play principle of *After the Fall,* but rather it serves to explain the reason that Quentin, after so many falls, cannot give himself up to despair. Unlike Tom Wingfield, Quentin holds a memory that includes a great deal of sympathy for the memories of others.

Tom Wingfield avoids all real contact with the other characters of the play, and he has genuine sympathy for only one, his sister Laura. Quentin, however, in spite of his first wife's complaints, is in close association with others. He is, to be sure, often in a struggle with them, but in each of his encounters—with Maggie, Louise, Rose, Felice, Lou, Mickey, Elsie, Barnes—he gives them his understanding and takes responsibility for their defeats. He is aware, of course, that he can fail others (as he does his father) without causing a defeat and he is, also, aware that he can try to help others (as he tries with Maggie) without insuring a success. But it is through his review of his relationships with his women—Louise, Maggie, and Holga—that Quentin is able to come to a workable conclusion: ". . . not certainty, I don't feel that. But it does seem feasible." . . .

In *After the Fall,* Quentin's memory does not have the absolute quality that Tom's memory has for him in *The Glass Menagerie. After the Fall* is a memory play, but it is a memory that the narrator accepts as a responsibility, not as a final authority.

The memory play as a kind of drama has so many advantages that it seems likely that there will be more of them. The danger of this genre is that it can give the playwright a sense of omniscience and

.that from the humble act of admitting or implying that all the world he knows is the one he remembers, he can leap to the assumption, or presumption, that the world of his memory is all the world there is. Williams, it seems, avoids such a leap in *The Glass Menagerie* on the narrowest grounds by making both the protagonist (Tom) and the antagonist (Amanda) morally inferior to the victim (Laura).

A second danger of this form is that it can lead to an abdication of responsibility with the assumption that memory is caused by events beyond the narrator's control. Critics who took Quentin's memory of Maggie as a biographical account of Miller's memory of Marilyn were offended and accused Miller of trying to "whitewash" himself in that relationship. Miller, it seems to me, does not "excuse or defend" his protagonist, but rather he makes Quentin responsible for his memory, not that it was formed, but responsible for what it will mean. When all is said and done, the audience for *After the Fall* has more sympathy for Maggie than Quentin has—but the audience's sympathy is a product of Miller's craftsmanship, not a denial of it.

One may easily identify the mechanical devices of a "memory play"—a single protagonist who serves as narrator; a sequence of actions selected from his memory to show his problem or demonstrate his nature; antagonists and supporting characters who exist only in relationship to the protagonist; a staging that borrows techniques from the expressionistic theatre; a method of dialogue, half-narrative in nature, personal in tone. These devices, however, are only the trappings of the form. The heart of the memory play is the dramatist's insistence that the most meaningful part of life is what is remembered, not what is done; and as such it is probably closer to romantic lyric poetry than to objective drama. It is a musing to be shared, not a debate to be judged.

Notes

[1]All citations from *The Glass Menagerie* are from the edition in Haskell M. Block and Robert G. Shedd's *Masters of Modern Drama* (New York, 1962), pp. 989–1017.
[2]All citations from this play are from Arthur Miller's *After the Fall* (New York, 1964).
[3]Michael Smith, "Review: *After the Fall,*" *The Village Voice,* January 30, 1964.
[4]"Arthur Miller: After the Silence," *Drama Survey,* IV (Fall, 1964), 520–30.
[5]*American Plays and Playwrights of the Contemporary Theatre* (New York, 1965), p. 37.

Notes on the Editor
and Contributors

R. B. PARKER is Professor of English at Trinity College in the University of Toronto, where he has served as chairman of the Graduate Drama Centre and of the Graduate English Program. His main field of scholarship is late Renaissance drama, but he has also edited contemporary Canadian plays and published articles on twentieth-century drama. He is currently chairman of the Editorial Advisory Board of *Modern Drama*.

J. BROOKS ATKINSON was drama critic of *The New York Times* for nearly thirty years, from 1921 to 1941 and from 1946 to 1960.

LESTER A. BEAURLINE, Professor of English at the University of Virginia, has published critical editions of plays by Jonson, Beaumont and Fletcher, Suckling, and Dryden, and is the author of a full-length critical study, *Jonson and Elizabethan Comedy* (1978).

JOHN STROTHER CLAYTON directed the graduate program of the University of North Carolina's Department of Radio, Television, and Motion Pictures, before becoming Principal Specialist in Educational Technology in the Department of Educational Affairs of the Organization of American States; currently, he is also president-elect of the International Division of the Association for Educational Communications and Technology. He has been consultant for educational television in seventeen countries and is the author of over one hundred media productions.

GILBERT DEBUSSCHER teaches English and American literature at the Free University, Brussels, and is past president of the Belgium-Luxembourg American Studies Association and secretary of the European Association for American Studies. He is the author of *Edward Albee: Tradition and Renewal* and several articles on Tennessee Williams, Jack Richardson, and avant garde drama. His *"The Glass Menagerie": York Notes* was published by Longmans in 1982.

FRANK DURHAM was Professor of American Literature and Modern Drama at the University of South Carolina from 1964 to 1971, after teaching at the Universities of Adelaide and Saigon. Among his publications are *Du Bose Heyward: The Man Who Wrote "Porgy"* (1954), the Twayne volume on *Elmer Rice,* and "Henry James' dramatization of his novels" in *James' "Daisy Miller": the Story, the Play, the Critics* (1963).

THOMAS L. KING is Associate Professor of Communication Arts in the theatre program of James Madison University, Virginia, where he teaches theatre history, dramatic literature and theory, and directs, designs, and acts in the production program. He has acted in several productions of *The Glass Menagerie.*

BENJAMIN NELSON is Professor of English and Comparative Literature at Fairleigh Dickinson University, New Jersey. Among his publications are books on *Tennessee Williams: The Man and His Work* (1961) and *Arthur Miller: Portrait of a Playwright* (1970).

PAUL T. NOLAN, the Dupré Professor of Humanities at the University of Southwestern Louisiana at Lafayette, has written over a hundred published plays (including *The Loneliest Game,* which won a National Players Workshop award) and is the author of several books about playwrights and plays, including studies of *Marc Connelly* and *John Wallace Crawford* for the Twayne series, *The Other Great Plays, Provincial Drama in America,* and *Three Full-Length Plays by John W. Crawford.*

JAMES L. ROWLANDS teaches in the Department of English at Washington State University at Pullman.

TOM SCANLAN is Associate Professor in the Department of Rhetoric at the University of Minnesota, St. Paul, where he teaches humanities and literature. He is the author of *Family, Drama, and American Dreams* (1978).

ROGER B. STEIN is Professor of Art History and English at the State University of New York at Binghamton. He has held Guggenheim and Fulbright fellowships, and is the author of *John Ruskin and Aesthetic Thought in America, 1840–1900* (1967), *Seascape and the*

American Imagination (1975), *Susquehanna: Images of a Settled Landscape* (1981), and other works.

HOWARD TAUBMAN, the author and editor of many books on theatre and music, followed Brooks Atkinson as drama critic for *The New York Times* from 1960 to 1966.

MAURICE YACOWAR is Dean of Humanities and Professor of Film Studies at Brock University, Ontario, Canada. Among his publications are: *Hitchcock's British Films* (1977), *Tennessee Williams and Film* (1977), *I Found It At The Movies* (1978), *Loser Takes All: the Comic Art of Woody Allen* (1979), and *Method in Madness: the Comic Art of Mel Brooks* (1981).

STARK YOUNG (1881–1963), novelist, playwright, director, and University teacher, served briefly as drama critic for *The New York Times* from 1924 to 1925 and for many years was a member of the editorial staffs of *The New Republic* and *Theatre Arts Monthly*. His reviews are collected in *Immortal Shadows, a Book of Dramatic Criticism (1922–1947)* (1948).

Chronology of Important Dates

1911   March 26: born Thomas Lanier Williams in Columbus, Mississippi.

1918   Family moved to St. Louis, Missouri.

1927   Article, "Can A Good Wife Be A Good Sport?", published in *Smart Set.*

1928   First story published in *Weird Tales.*

1929   Entered University of Missouri. Won prizes for prose, poetry, and a play.

1931   Withdrawn from university and put to work in International Shoe Co. Warehouse; wrote at home at night.

1935   After breakdown, spent year recuperating with grandparents in Memphis. First play, *Cairo! Shanghai! Bombay!* produced.

1936   Entered Washington University, St. Louis. *The Magic Tower* and *Headlines* produced.

1937   Entered University of Iowa. *Candles to the Sun* and *The Fugitive Kind* (different from the movie) produced. Rose's prefrontal lobotomy.

1938   Graduated from Iowa. Wrote *Not About Nightingales.*

1939   Itinerant writer. Won Group Theatre prize for *American Blues.* Awarded Rockefeller grant.

1940   Entered John Gassner's playwriting class in New York. *Battle of Angels* failed in Boston.

1941–42 Resumed life as itinerant writer.

1943   Hired as MGM scriptwriter in California.

1943   *You Touched Me,* by Williams and Donald Windham, produced.

1944   *The Glass Menagerie* opened in Chicago, December 26.

1945   *The Glass Menagerie* produced at the Playhouse, New York, won the New York Critics' Circle award, and was published by Random House. Fourth unsuccessful operation for cataract.

1946   *27 Wagons Full of Cotton and Other Plays* published.

1947   *Stairs to the Roof* produced in Pasadena; *Summer and Smoke* produced in Chicago; *A Streetcar Named Desire* produced in New York, won second New York Critics' Circle Award and Pulitzer Prize, and published by New Directions.

1948   *Summer and Smoke* produced in New York. One act plays, *American Blues,* and short stories, *One Arm and Other Stories,* published. *The Glass Menagerie* produced in London.

1950   Novel, *The Roman Spring of Mrs. Stone* published. Film, *The Glass Menagerie* released.

1951   *The Rose Tattoo* produced in New York, won Tony Award. *I Rise in Flame, Cried the Phoenix* published. Film, *A Streetcar Named Desire* released.

1953   *Camino Real* produced in New York.

1954   Short stories, *Hard Candy,* published.

1955   *Cat on a Hot Tin Roof* produced in New York, won third New York Critics' Circle Award and second Pulitzer Prize. *Glass Menagerie* revived in New York. Film, *The Rose Tattoo* released.

1956   *Sweet Bird of Youth* produced in Miami. Film, *Baby Doll* released. Poems, *In the Winter of Cities,* published.

1957   *Orpheus Descending* (revision of *Battle of Angels*) produced in New York. Williams began psychoanalysis.

1958   *Garden District (Something Unspoken* and *Suddenly Last Summer)* produced Off-Broadway. *Period of Adjustment* produced in Miami. Film of *Cat* released.

1959   *Sweet Bird of Youth* produced in New York. Film, *Suddenly Last Summer* released. *The Night of the Iguana* produced at Spoleto.

1960   *Period of Adjustment* produced in New York. Film, *The Fugitive Kind* (screen version of *Orpheus Descending*) released.

1961   *The Night of the Iguana* produced in New York, won 4th New York Critics' Circle Award. Theatre Guild tour of *The Glass Menagerie.* Films of *The Roman Spring of Mrs. Stone* and *Summer and Smoke* released.

1962   First version of *The Milk Train Doesn't Stop Here Anymore* produced at Spoleto. Films of *Sweet Bird of Youth* and *Period of Adjustment* released.

1963   Second version of *Milk Train* produced in New York. Donated papers to the University of Texas. Death of Frank Merlo threw Williams into depression.

1964   First version of *The Eccentricities of a Nightingale* produced in summer stock. Film of *Night of the Iguana* released. *The Glass Menagerie* produced at Minneapolis and Caedmon recording released.

1965   *The Glass Menagerie* revived in New York.

1966   *Slapstick Tragedy (The Mutilated* and *The Gnädiges Fräulein)* failed in New York. *The Glass Menagerie* and the early version of *Camino Real* televised. Film, *This Property is Condemned* released.

1967   First version of *The Two-Character Play* produced in Hampstead, London. *The Knightly Quest: a Novella and Four Short Stories* published.

1968   *Kingdom of Earth (The Seven Descents of Myrtle)* produced in New York. Film, *Boom!* released.

1969   *In the Bar of a Tokyo Hotel* failed Off-Broadway. Film, *Last of the Mobile Hot-Shots* released. Williams converted to Roman Catholicism, spent three months in St. Louis hospital after breakdown in Key West.

1970   *Dragon Country: A Book of Plays* published.

1971   Second version of *Two-Character Play* (titled *Out Cry*) produced in Chicago. First volume of the collected *The Theatre of Tennessee Williams* published by New Directions (vol. 7 completed in 1981).

1972   *Small Craft Warnings* produced successfully Off-Off-Broadway, and published.

1973   Third version of *Two-Character Play* (titled *Out Cry*) failed in New York. *The Glass Menagerie* again televised. Harry Rasky's CBC special "Tennessee Williams' South" televised. *Out Cry* published.

1974   *Eight Mortal Ladies Possessed: A Book of Stories* published. *The Latter Days of a Celebrated Soubrette* produced in New York. *The Migrants* televised.

1975   First version of *The Red Devil Battery Sign* failed in Boston. Fourth version of *The Two-Character Play* produced Off-Off-Broadway. *The Glass Menagerie* revived in New York. Novel, *Moise and the World of Reason* and *Memoirs* published.

1976   Second version of *Red Devil* produced in Vienna. *This Is (An Entertainment)* produced in San Francisco. Second version of *Eccentricities of a Nightingale* produced in Buffalo and New York. *Eccentricities* and *Cat* televised. *Letters to Donald Windham* published.

1977   *Vieux Carré* produced in New York. *The Glass Menagerie* revived in London. Poems *Androgyne, Mon Amour* published.

1978   *Tiger Tale* produced in Atlanta. *Crève Coeur* produced in Charleston. Essays, *Where I Live* and Richard Leavitt, ed., *The World of Tennessee Williams* published.

1979   *The Two-Character Play* published. *Vieux Carré* published.

1980   *Clothes for a Summer Hotel* failed on Broadway. *Crève Coeur* published.

1981   *The Notebooks of Trigorin* produced in Vancouver; *A House Not Meant To Stand* produced in Chicago; *Something Cloudy, Something Clear* produced Off-Off-Broadway.

1983   Died in New York, February 26.

Supplementary Bibliography

I. Bibliographical

The "reading edition" of *The Glass Menagerie* is published by New Directions, and is reprinted in volume I of *The Theatre of Tennessee Williams* (New Directions, 1971); the "acting edition" is published by the Dramatists Play Service. Recent works on or by Williams are incorporated into Charles A. Carpenter Jr's annual bibliographies for *Modern Drama,* and a twice-yearly newsletter, *The Tennessee Williams Review* (Ann Arbor: University of Michigan, Spring, 1979—), is edited by Stephen Stanton.

The main research tool is: Drewey Wayne Gunn. *Tennessee Williams: A Bibliography* (Metuchen, N.J.: Scarecrow Press, 1980), which can be used with the following:

BROWN, ANDREAS. "Tennessee Williams By Another Name," *Papers of the Bibliographical Society of America,* 57 (1963), 377–8.

CARPENTER, CHARLES A., JR. and ELIZABETH COOK, "Addenda to Tennessee Williams: A Selected Bibliography," *Modern Drama,* 2 (December 1959) 220–3.

DONY, NADINE. "Tennessee Williams: A Selected Bibliography," *Modern Drama,* 1 (December 1958), 181–91.

GUNN, DREWEY WAYNE. "The Various Texts of Tennessee Williams' Plays," *Educational Theatre Journal,* 30 (October 1978), 368–75.

LITTO, FREDERIC. *American Dissertations on the Drama and the Theatre: A Bibliography.* Kent, Ohio: Kent State University Press, 1969.

PRESLEY, DELMA E. "Tennessee Williams: Twenty-five Years of Criticism," *Bulletin of Bibliography,* 30 (Jan.-March 1973), 21–9.

II. Material on Williams' Life and Approach to Writing

ANONYMOUS, "The Life and Ideas of Tennessee Williams," *New York PM Magazine,* May 6, 1945, pp. 6 ff.

BARNETT, LINCOLN. "Tennessee Williams," *Life,* 24 (February 16, 1948),

113–27 (reprinted in *Writings on Life: Sixteen Close-Ups.* New York: William Sloane, 1951).

COURTNEY, MARGUERITE. *Laurette.* (New York: Rinehart, 1955)—a biography of Laurette Taylor.

FUNKE, LEWIS, and JOHN E. BOOTH. "Williams on Williams," *Theatre Arts,* 46 (January 1962), 16–19, 72–3.

HUGHES, CATHARINE. *Tennessee Williams: A Biography*—forthcoming from Prentice-Hall, Inc.

LEAVITT, RICHARD F., ed. *The World of Tennessee Williams.* New York: G.P. Putnam's Sons, 1978.

LEWIS, R. C., "A Playwright Named Tennessee," *New York Times Magazine,* December 7, 1947, pp. 19, 67–70.

MOOR, PAUL. "A Mississippian Named Tennessee," *Harper's,* 197 (July 1948), 63–71.

STANG, JOANNE. "Williams: 20 Years After 'Glass Menagerie'," *New York Times,* March 28, 1965, sec. 2, pp. 1, 3.

STEEN, MIKE. *A Look at Tennessee Williams.* New York: Hawthorn, 1969— note especially the interviews with Irving Rapper, William Inge, Paul Bowles, and Maureen Stapleton.

WILLIAMS, EDWINA DAKIN, as told to Lucy Freeman. *Remember Me to Tom.* New York: G.P. Putnam's Sons, 1963.

WILLIAMS, TENNESSEE. "Laurette Taylor, An Appreciation." *New York Times,* December 15, 1946, sec. 2, p. 4.

WILLIAMS, TENNESSEE. *Memoirs.* New York: Doubleday and Co., Inc., 1975.

WILLIAMS, TENNESSEE. *Letters to Donald Windham, 1940–1965,* ed. Donald Windham. New York: Holt, Rinehart and Winston, 1977.

WILLIAMS, TENNESSEE. *Where I Live. Selected Essays,* ed. Christine R. Day and Bob Woods. New York: New Directions, 1978.

III. Critical Writings

BEAURLINE, LESTER A. "The Director, the Script, and the Author's Revisions: A Critical Problem," in *Papers on Dramatic Theory and Criticism,* ed. David M. Knauf. Iowa: University of Iowa Press, 1969, pp. 88ff.

BERKOWITZ, GERALD M. "The 'Other World' of *The Glass Menagerie,*" *Players,* 48 (April–May 1973), 150–3.

BLUEFARB, SAM. *"The Glass Menagerie:* Three Visions of Time," *College English,* 24 (April 1963), 513–18.

BRANDT, GEORGE. "Cinematic Structure in the Works of Tennessee Williams," *American Theatre* (Stratford-upon-Avon Studies), ed. J. R. Brown and B. Harris. London: Edward Arnold, 1967, pp. 163–87.

BROWN, RAY C. B. "Tennessee Williams: The Poetry of Stagecraft," *Voices,* 138 (1949), 4.

CALLAHAN, EDWARD F. "Tennessee Williams' Two Worlds," *North Dakota Quarterly,* 25 (Summer 1957), 61–67.

CASTY, ALAN. "Tennessee Williams and the Small Hands of the Rain," *Mad River Review,* I (Fall–Winter 1965), 27–43.

CATE, HOLLIS C. and DELMA E. PRESLEY, "Beyond Stereotype: Ambiguity in Amanda Wingfield," *Notes on Mississippi Writers,* 3 (Winter 1971), 91–100.

CHICK, NANCY A. "Showing and telling: narrators in the drama of Tennessee Williams," *American Literature,* 51 (1979), 84–93.

COHN, RUBY. *Dialogue in American Drama.* Bloomington: Indiana University Press, 1971, pp. 97–129.

CORRIGAN, MARY ANN. "Beyond Verisimilitude: Echoes of Expressionism in Williams' Plays," in Tharpe, *(q v.),* pp. 375 ff.

CORRIGAN, MARY ANN. "Memory, Dream and Myth in the Plays of Tennessee Williams," *Renascence,* 28 (Spring 1976), 155–67.

DAVIS, JOSEPH K. "The American South as Mediating Image in the Plays of Tennessee Williams," *Amerikanisches Drama und Theater in 20 Jahrhundert,* eds. Alfred Weber and Siegfried Neuweiler. Gottingen: Vandenhoeck, 1976, pp. 171–89.

DEBUSSCHER, GILBERT. "Tennessee Williams's Unicorn Broken Again," *Revue belge de Philologie et d'Histoire,* 49 (1971), 875–85.

DEBUSSCHER, GILBERT. *York Notes on Tennessee Williams. "The Glass Menagerie."* (London: Longman, York Press, 1982.)

DONAHUE, FRANCIS. *The Dramatic World of Tennessee Williams.* New York: Frederick Ungar, 1964.

ELLIS, BROBURY PEARCE. " 'The True Original Copies' " [on the composition of *The Glass Menagerie*], *Tulane Drama Review,* 5 (September 1960), 113–16.

FALK, SIGNI LENEA. *Tennessee Williams* (Twayne's United States Authors Series). New York: Twayne, 1962. Second edition, 1978.

FEDDER, NORMAN J. *The Influence of D. H. Lawrence on Tennessee Williams.* (Studies in American Literature). The Hague: Mouton, 1966.

GANZ, ARTHUR. "The Desperate Morality of the Plays of Tennessee Williams," *American Scholar,* 31 (Spring 1962), 278–94.

HIRSCH, FOSTER. *A Portrait of the Artist: The Plays of Tennessee Williams.* Port Washington, N.Y.: Kennikat, 1978.

HONORS ENGLISH 11-1 (1966–67), Roy C. Ketcham Senior High School, Wappingers Falls, N.Y. "Through a Glass Starkly." *English Journal,* 57 (February 1968), 209–12, 220.

HOWELL, ELMO. "The Function of Gentlemen Callers: A Note on Tennessee Williams' *The Glass Menagerie,*" *Notes on Mississippi Writers,* 2 (Winter 1970), 83–90.

JACKSON, ESTHER MERLE. *The Broken World of Tennessee Williams.* Madison: University of Wisconsin Press, 1965.

JONES, ROBERT EMMET. "Tennessee Williams's Early Heroines." *Modern Drama,* 2 (December 1959), 211–19.

JOVEN, NILDA G. "Illusion and Reality in Tennessee Williams' *The Glass Menagerie,*" *Dillman Review,* 14 (January 1966), 81–89.

KAHN, SY. "Through a Glass Menagerie Darkly: the World of Tennessee Williams," *Modern American Drama: Essays in Criticism,* ed. William E. Taylor. De Land, Fla.: Everett-Edwards, 1968.

KRAMER, VICTOR A. "Memoirs of Self-Indictment: The Solitude of Tennessee Williams," in Tharpe, pp. 663–75.

LAWRENCE, ELAINE LOUISE. "Four Defeated Heroines: Tennessee Williams' Southern Gentlewomen," *Lit,* 7 (Spring 1966), 7–39.

LEES, DANIEL E. *"The Glass Menagerie:* A Black *Cinderella,"* Unisa English Studies, 11 (March 1973), 30–4.

LUHR, FRIEDRICH WILHELM. "The Glass Menagerie," in *Zeitgenössische amerikanische Dichtung,* ed. Werner Huller, *et al.* (Frankfurt, 1969), 147–58: [in German].

MACMULLAN, HUGH. "Translating 'The Glass Menagerie' to Film," *Hollywood Quarterly,* 5 (Fall 1950), 14–32.

MIELZINER, JO. "Scene Designs for *The Glass Menagerie,*" *Theatre Arts,* 29 (April 1945), 211.

NAPIERALSKI, EDMUND A. "Tennessee Williams' *The Glass Menagerie:* the Dramatic Metaphor," *Southern Quarterly,* 16 (1977), 1–12.

NATHAN, GEORGE JEAN. *Theater Book of The Year, 1944–45*. New York: Knopf, 1945, pp. 324–7.

NIESEN, GEORGE. "The Artist against the Reality in the Plays of Tennessee Williams," in Tharpe, pp. 463 ff.

NYSZKIEWICZ, HEINZ. "Drama, Bild und Wort in Tennessee Williams' 'Glassmenagerie'." *Die Pädagogische Provinz,* 17 (1963), 308–20: [in German].

PAVLOV, GRIGOR. "A Comparative Study of Tennessee Williams' *The Glass Menagerie* and *Portrait of a Girl in Glass,*" *Annuaire de l'Université de Sofie,* Faculté des Lettres, 62 (1968), 111–31.

PHILLIPS, GENE D. *The Films of Tennessee Williams.* East Brunswick, N.J.: Associated University Presses, 1980.

RAMA MURTHY, V. *American Expressionistic Drama, Containing Analyses of Three Outstanding American Plays: O'Neill, The Hairy Ape; Tennessee Williams, The Glass Menagerie; Miller, Death of a Salesman.* Delhi: Doaba House, 1970.

RIBEY, CORA. "Chloroses—Pâles Roses and Pleurosis—Blue Roses," *Romance Notes,* 13 (1971), 250–1 [Traces the conceit to Baudelaire's *Fleurs du Mal*].

ROGERS, INGRID. *Tennessee Williams: A Moralist's Answer to the Perils of Life.* Frankfurt: M.P. Lang, 1976.

STANTON, STEPHEN, ed. *Tennessee Williams: A Collection of Critical Essays.* Englewood Cliffs, N.J.: Prentice-Hall, 1977.

STAVROU, CONSTANTINE N. "The Neurotic Heroine in Tennessee Williams," *Literature and Psychology,* 5 (May 1955), 26–34.

THARPE, JAC, ed. *Tennessee Williams: A Tribute.* Jackson: University Press of Mississippi, 1977.

THOMPSON, JUDITH. "Symbol, Myth, and Ritual in *The Glass Menagerie, The Rose Tattoo,* and *Orpheus Descending,*" in Tharpe, pp. 679–711.

TISCHLER, NANCY. "The Distorted Mirror: Tennessee Williams' Self-Press, 1961.

TISCHLER, NANCY. "The Distorted Mirror: Tennessee Williams' Self-Portraits," *Mississippi Quarterly,* 25 (1972), 389–403 (reprinted in Stanton).

WATSON, CHARLES S. "The Revision of *The Glass Menagerie:* The Passing of Good Manners," *Southern Literary Journal,* 8 (Spring 1976), 74–8.

WEALES, GERARD. *Tennessee Williams.* (University of Minnesota Pamphlets on American Writers). Minneapolis: University of Minnesota Press, 1965; revised 1974.

WELLS, ARVIN R. "The Glass Menagerie," in *Insight,* ed. John V. Hagopian and Martin Doch. Frankfurt: Hirschgraben–Verlag, 1967. I, 272–80.